MW00653052

"Integral healing has found an innovative thinker in Diane Tegtmeier. *Relationships That Heal* is a MUST READ for anyone who practices healing in today's world."

Peter Amato, CEO, Inner Harmony Group

"This book provides a model that will challenge—in a compassionate, deeply thoughtful and human way—everything you thought you knew about the professional helping relationship."

Dorothy Van Soest, PhD, MSW,
Professor and former Dean, University of Washington

"Relationship is the crucible of humanity's evolution to the heart chakra. Through personal stories, here is a manual that shows how to navigate the many dynamics of therapeutic relationships and maximize the healing power of love."

Anodea Judith,
Author of *Waking the Global Heart*

"In her new volume *Relationships that Heal*, environmental activist, clinical social worker and energy practitioner Diane Tegtmeier has succeeded in explicating and integrating a deeply-colored, varied, and extensive amount of material. Her work draws broadly upon the cell membrane model to illustrate crucial ecological ideas of wholeness, interconnectedness and permeability. Tegtmeier's book is highly readable, richly metaphorical and imminently practical. It includes abundant examples from her own life and practice experience that will assist the interested reader and professional practitioner alike in understanding and applying these concepts to a wide-range of helping contexts."

Fred H. Besthorn, M.Div., MSW, Ph.D.
Associate Professor of Social Work
University of Northern Iowa

"Relationships That Heal is an awakening to nature's universal healing dynamics! Tegtmeier spells out the practical steps for navigating a healing partnership in a way that translates seamlessly to my methodologies. It gives meaningful context for my true role in the healing arts."

Shaw Coté, Cranio-Sacral and Massage Therapist,

"Tegtmeier offers a new point of view of sexuality—not an anthropocentric, but an ecocentric one. Here we have a guide to dealing with sexual issues in counseling and therapeutic processes that enable us to become more aware of our co-creative relationship with all life in Earth, honouring our power, and becoming more responsible toward ourselves and others."

Marcella Danon,
Vice-President of the European Ecopsychology Society

"Using the cell membrane model, Diane has created a clear set of tools that are proving to be invaluable in my practice. She lays out guidelines that not only offer insight to shift uncomfortable situations, but also allow healing energy to enter."

Patti Phillips, Aquatic Bodywork Practitioner,
Massage Therapist and Physical Therapy Assistant.

"Diane Tegtmeier has written a wonderful book that will be of benefit to any practitioner who enters into healing relationships. She very cleverly uses the physiology of cell membranes to describe methods of fostering ethical interactions with our clients/patients.

"Diane also draws on her experiences to illustrate how good intentions alone may not adequately serve our patients/clients as well as not adequately protect us caregivers from charges of ethical violations. I foresee that the use of this book in the teaching setting by faculty and students in various disciplines of the Healing Arts will stimulate healthy discussions which will result in grounded, centered students. They will be well prepared to deal with the complex issues that may arise in the course of being involved in healing relationships."

Robert D. McKay MD,
Anesthesiologist and Pain Management physician, Watsu Practitioner,
Therapeutic Yoga Practitioner, Bristol Tennessee

NATURAL ETHICS FOR TODAY'S HEALTH PRACTITIONER

RELATIONSHIPS
THAT
HEAL

Skillful Practice within Nature's Web

DIANE TEGTMEIER, MSW, NCTMB

ISBN 0-7414-5520-X

Poem excerpt, page 190, Reprinted from *Call Me By My True Names* (1999) by Thich Nhat Hanh with permission of Parallax Press, Berkeley, California, www.parallax.org.

Cover Art (circular drawing) by Ruth Richards, copyright 2009.

Cover photograph by Diane Tegtmeier

Author photograph by Andrew Yavelow

Interior Illustrations collaboratively designed by Bob Oertel, Ruth Richards and Inika Spence.

Copyedit: Dan Barth

Writing Coach: Hal Zina Bennett

Typeset and layout: Jim Gilkeson

Published by:

1094 New DeHaven Street, Suite 100
West Conshohocken, PA 19428-2713
Info@buybooksontheweb.com
www.buybooksontheweb.com
Toll-free (877) BUY BOOK
Local Phone (610) 941-9999
Fax (610) 941-9959

Printed in the United States of America
Published October 2009
Printed on recycled paper

In loving memory
of Mom
and in dedication to
Bella, Owen, Lily and Barrett

TABLE OF CONTENTS

PROLOGUE

Where are the boundaries between river and sea, where gulls gather to feast upon the richness at the interface? When water and sand meet, each changes the other, moment by moment by moment. You know that river, sea, waves and shore are different from each other, yet where are the boundaries between them? There are no boundaries in nature, only interactive fields of relationship. How does nature manage the complex relationships formed as the edge of one system touches another?

I'm sitting at the edge of the North American continent at what was once the easternmost edge of the Russian Empire—Fort Ross, California. Just south of here the Russian River meets the Pacific Ocean. The nature of the relationship formed as one ecosystem meets another profoundly affects the health of both. Each is a world of its own, nurturing, sustaining and healing itself as part of the larger living, breathing web of life. All ecosystems and cultures touch others. In the places where they meet, each experiences a bit of the other, to stretch beyond familiar patterns and possibly to grow. Awareness is heightened at the edge. Here at Fort Ross, Russians, Spaniards and Native Americans met at culture's edge. Today, threads of all these peoples are woven into the evolving landscape and culture of this place.

Healing relationships are like the meetings between ecosystems, organisms and the cells of all living things. Nature repeats patterns throughout all dimensions of life. It is in meeting or touching another that we can both discover and express who we are. In the interface between client and therapist, we may be called upon to shift and grow, to learn and discover. We come together and often bring each other to the edge of what we know about ourselves and what's ready to heal. Patterns lying deep within come to the surface, like shells brought from the ocean's depth as waves meet the shore. We risk change when we come to our edge and invite others to theirs.

This book invites you to step more consciously into nature's web as you touch another in healing.

Come to the Edge the voice said softly
No they said it's too high
Come to the edge the voice insisted
No she said it's too dangerous
Come to the edge the voice demanded
No he said I might fall
Come to the edge the voice commanded
Reluctantly, I came to the edge
He pushed me off
And I flew

Charles Logue

An Invitation to Nature's Model for Healing Presence

A wounded body, heart and spirit heal best in the compassionate presence of another, and that is what this book is about. What does it take to be fully present with another in the face of illness and pain? What would it take to make the relationship itself the container for healing? If you've come to this book, it's probably because you've asked yourself similar questions as you join with others to support healing and bring comfort. If your practice embraces the interconnected nature of the physical, emotional, social and spiritual, you may be seeking a healing relationship model that fits your holistic practice. You've likely witnessed those magical or mystical moments where what happens between you and your client seems to matter as much or more than the technique you're applying—situations that ask for your compassionate presence. This book is about those moments and it offers a perspective that may help you answer these important questions.

I thought I knew at least some of the answers to those questions as I sat on the edge of a cliff overlooking the Pacific Ocean and started to write this book. I had been teaching a natural model for ethics to bodywork students for a time, and had a good idea what I wanted to write. I retreated to this favorite coastal spot at Fort Ross, California, away from my usual distractions. As I settled into a ground chair, computer in my lap, the grandeur and mystery of the place expanded before my eyes. "If nature is to be your guide in being with another in healing," the landscape seemed to say, "then look closely and listen." I did. The mystery of relationship in nature revealed itself anew to me, and thus began the healing and learning journey this book would become.

Oh, that I could have just stayed in that pristine landscape to finish the book! No, like all good healing relationships, this book took me out of the safety of what I thought I knew and into the interface between that and what I was about to learn while writing. The book itself and the natural principles I attempted to reveal kept working on me. They demanded that I walk them through the labyrinth of the relationships I formed with those I wanted to help in my integrative bodywork practice.

I tried to quit writing the book many times. I'd much rather read a book than write one. You know how it is when you try to back out of a relationship— it keeps coming at you until you make peace with it. I knew that writing the book was making me a better therapist; it could do the same for you. This book is both a reflective and an instructive journey, which I hope will guide you into your own reflections. As you become the fly on the wall of my treatment space and learn how nature guides me through the promise and pitfalls of a healing relationship, I hope you gain a better idea of what it is you're doing in your own. Perhaps more important, I hope it will help you learn more about yourself and who you are when you're in a healing relationship.

I travelled many different paths in my education and career development around relationships and ethics:

- As a graduate student in social work over 25 years ago each class included extensive teaching of ethics and many different perspectives on the client/worker relationship.

- Long before that, however, I was steeped in the ethics of scientific research. Within the boundaries of the disciplines of microbiology, physiology and chemistry I learned about the relationships among and within atoms, molecules, cells and organs.

- The subsequent study of ecology profoundly expanded my understanding of the relationship arena to include the relationships among all living things and the planetary home in which we co-evolved.

- As an environmental activist and organizer I observed power relationships in the political arena and the attempts to restrain its abuses through law and ethics.

- Later, in my own therapy, I saw how my family functioned much like an ecosystem, each member doing its part in the co-evolution of the family and culture.

- After years working as a social worker in hospitals, the study of subtle energy healing expanded my perception of living systems and how they relate to each other even more.

The many manifestations of relationship dynamics, therefore, have been the common thread in much of my personal and professional inquiry. Whether I was learning about the relationships among atoms or cells in living tissue or humans in their social environment, the common patterns of relationship in nature slowly shaped my consciousness around our interactions with each other.

Throughout this multi-faceted career development, there was no single incident that made me aware of the limitations of conventional ethics in guiding my relationships with clients. When I got stuck and didn't quite know what to do in a challenging situation, however, I noticed that I was increasingly seeking guidance from nature as much as the standards of practice. Sometimes that guidance came as I walked in the prairie or some other wild place away from the client relationship, but there was more to come.

When colleagues and teachers talked about boundaries, I'd feel uncomfortable and wasn't sure why. When what I understood about boundaries wasn't fitting a particularly difficult situation in my practice my mind would often travel to what Dr. Tommy Dunnagan, my cell physiology professor, used to say about the selectively permeable cell membrane of all living things. I remembered how it both contained the cell and kept it organized, but also served as the traffic cop for what went in and out of the cell and when. Back in 1963, I thought Tommy was obsessed with the cell membrane; he talked about it over and over again. I wanted him to get to the hot topic of the day—the recently discovered double helix of the genetic code all coiled up in the nucleus and in charge of everything! Decades later, I realized Tommy was really on to something. In 2005, Bruce Lipton referred to the "magical mem-Brain" in his book, *The Biology of Belief.* He described how DNA needs the cell membrane to tell it what's going on outside the cell. The membrane both protects and informs the DNA in the cell's center, giving the cell "awareness." As I found myself in power struggles with clients, the cell membrane started to talk to me again, and now I listened more attentively.

That day at Fort Ross, I marveled at how this elegant structure of the cell membrane was managing all the relationships within that landscape to keep everything in healthy balance. All of the communication, nurture and healing going on all around me followed the principles by which the cell membrane functions in all living things. In this book, I describe how these principles of containment, selective permeability, differentiation, interspace, centering and Oneness revealed themselves to me and led me into more skillful healing relationships.

You may have been in professional practice for a while and learned the value of honoring your own boundaries and those of your clients in a relationship. Or you may be new to a helping profession and are just learning your way around the healing relationship minefield with the code of ethics as your map. With these basics in place, however, you may be looking beyond them to increase your overall effectiveness as a therapist through improved relationship skills that match your holistic practice. Even though you may be quite skilled in the technique of your practice, you may be finding that you'd like to be more skillful in the way you respond when something uncomfortable happens in a relationship that blocks what you're trying to do. You may find yourself wanting to yell, "Help!" in tough situations. If you're licensed to talk with your clients, and you are called to touch them (or vice versa), do your professional standards offer the guidance you need when the scope of practice defined for you begins to constrain your creativity and growth? Would better relationship skills help you either sleep better at night or at least know what to do when you feel like your client is moving around in your gut as you sleep? If you feel prodded to grow in your ability to be a healing presence for others, this book offers support. It was at times like these and many others when I found guidance in the way the cell membrane responds to what's happening around it. I offer the model I've derived from that guidance as a way to help you create more effective healing relationships.

These days a good part of my practice involves holding people close to my heart in a pool of spring water warmed by the earth in an aquatic bodywork practice. I move them in the rhythm of their own breath, while I entrain my breath to theirs. I bring as much consciousness as I'm capable of in the moment to whatever is happening in their body, mind, heart and spirit while I employ and integrate all of the techniques (in both talk and touch) I've learned over the years to facilitate healing. The intimacy of such a practice puts the validity of the cell membrane model through a pretty demanding test. Whenever a healing relationship works well, I see how the principles of the cell membrane are at work. Whenever I make a mistake, these same principles point me to how and why, and I continue to grow in awareness of the mystery of the healing relationship. Wherever you are in your development as a practitioner, the cell membrane can also help you in that development.

I invite you to join me on this new kind of inquiry into professional ethics. Such an inquiry doesn't yield prescriptive dos and don'ts like conventional codes of ethics, nor will each relationship situation point directly to "what nature would do." This inquiry into natural ethics won't yield quick or easy answers that neatly fit into an old mechanical model of nature. Nature is very good at confounding human attempts at controlling or predicting just what will happen, and sometimes things can get quite messy and sticky. However, if through this inquiry you step more consciously into nature's evolutionary dance, it's more likely that you and your healing partners can achieve co-creative outcomes in healing, with nature's relationship manager, the cell membrane, for help.

In these chapters, I reflect upon my own experiences and how nature and the cell membrane inspire my professional relationships. While I offer tips throughout the book on how nature's model can inspire and guide your healing relationships, the point of this book is not to show you exactly how the cell membrane model will work in your practice situations. Instead, by showing how these principles inspire my work, I invite your consciousness and healing responses to grow and evolve with clients as nature does—relationship by relationship. This inquiry into nature's ethics may lead you beyond your assumptions of where the power lies in healing relationships and into a new model that's as old as life on Earth. No matter what your field of practice, the cell membrane model affords you and your clients the same safety as clearly set boundaries, while also creating a space in which you can both learn and grow. I offer a five-step process that arises out of nature's model that can guide you through those difficult situations you encounter in your practice. This process can be practiced both within and outside of sessions to support a healing response. Later in the book, I'll show how the model can be applied to common areas of ethical consideration: creating a safe space, power, money, dual relationships and sexuality.

The names I use throughout the text are not the person's real name, and in fact, some of the healing stories I tell are composites of the actual ones. In so doing, I intend to tell the truth of the experience, but prevent the facts from violating the trust and confidence of those who helped me understand the nature of our relationships. I've changed the gender of some of the persons in these stories as well, and have freely used the masculine and feminine pronouns to avoid the cumbersome his/her and s/he notations. If you recognize yourself in these pages, please know that by tapping into the healing process of someone like you, we've tapped into all.

In this book, we will learn to step into and not resist the evolutionary process unfolding in the healing arts professions, as well.

The boundaries between the sciences that inform medicine today are falling. We now have a field called "psychoneuroimmunology," for example, and research papers try to measure "biopsychosocial" parameters. Even science and spirituality are finding common ground as we co-creatively weave new integral models of healing. The cell membrane model I describe in this book takes us beyond the concept of boundaries into a perspective on the healing relationship that serves this evolving paradigm of integral healing. It offers you the opportunity to expand your consciousness around a healing relationship to meet the demands of such a paradigm.

We have an opportunity, when we meet another with the intention to heal, to align our practices with the evolutionary process of all life, and in so doing become a more healing presence for those who come to us for help. We can learn to embrace the challenge for change that these relationships offer, like the waves that touch the shore at Fort Ross.

SECTION 1

The Cell Membrane Model for Healing Relationships

NATURE, HEALING AND THE HEALING RELATIONSHIP

"If you do not rest upon the good foundation of nature, you will labor with little honor and less profit. Those who take for their standard anyone but nature—the mistress of all masters—weary themselves in vain."

Leonardo daVinci (1452-1519)

What I see when I look to nature for a standard is what I'm attuned to see. The consciousness with which I observe nature has developed all through my life, through both direct experience and scientific study. Yet, when I attempt to take nature as a standard for the healing relationship, I run the same risk clerics and politicians do when they use scripture to support their ideas about managing relationships. Even though we might intuitively sense the wisdom in what Leonardo daVinci advised so long ago, how can anyone pretend to really know what nature's standard is? We usually see only what we're attuned to seeing and often select as truth only that which supports our current vision.

In one of my workshops on the healing relationship, a student countered my thoughts on nature as a model with, "There's violence in nature! Female animals get raped all the time!" She is a woman who had been treated badly all her life by men acting out their idea of nature, and she wasn't buying my more benevolent view of

1

nature. So, the consciousness with which we interpret nature, or even sacred scripture, is shaped by the emotions and history of the one doing the interpreting. Later, I'll describe how that very process of interpretation is explained by the selective permeability of the cell membrane. For now, however, it's important that I state where I'm coming from as I define healing and the healing relationship using nature's standard. I focus on the basic concepts of wholeness, interconnection, collaboration, homeostasis, the evolutionary process and transformation to frame my picture of healing in nature.

Wholeness and Interconnection

I have returned to Fort Ross often on this inquiry into nature's model. From my cliffside perch I watch waves crash into rocks, pelicans glide overhead and sea lions lumber their way on to an island of stone they share with cormorants, terns and gulls. I listen to the calls and songs of the birds as the sea lions bark to each other amidst the sound of the breaking surf. My human consciousness projects all kinds of meanings on what I sense happening around me. In time, however, my consciousness moves beyond the need to know meaning, and I drop into the awareness of being One with the sea sounds. Each cell of my body feels at peace in intimacy with this place; I feel healed.

Violence is here, too, as my student points out. The cute sea otter is pulverizing a mussel, a shelled living animal, against its breastbone, pulling its tender flesh from its protective shell and eating it live. Countless numbers of animals are eating each other within the seascape that brings me to a state of peace that I call beautiful. Words like "violence," "cute," "protective," and "beautiful" arise out of human consciousness and our tendency to place a value on what we see. That I could feel such peace in the presence of what we call violence brings me to the challenge I've given myself in using nature as a guide for the healing relationship. Isn't a nice, crisp, clearly articulated code of ethics a more reliable vehicle for this? In trying to answer that question, I remember a talk I heard by Matthew Fox in describing his approach to Creation Spirituality. He said that all of creation is beautiful, but not always pretty. He asked us to imagine an eagle swooping down to snatch a baby bunny in its talons. It wasn't a pretty sight, he said, especially if you're the bunny. Shoulders hunched and little squeals erupted among the urban audience. But beautiful is different from pretty, he noted. Beauty and healing in nature encompass the whole. Healing supports the balance of the bunny population that is maintained by predators who are at the same time protecting the vegetation on which they all depend.

I'm not endorsing predatory behavior with your patients and clients, but I make the point in order to illustrate how the concepts of wholeness and interconnectedness are integral to our understanding of healing in nature. In order for me to feel whole and at peace in the face of what could be perceived as violence taking place around me, my consciousness had to expand to include both the beauty of the birds' song and the crushed mussel as part of a wondrous whole, the complexity of which I can only begin to grasp.

When we stand beside another in pain with intention to heal, we have an opportunity to expand our awareness to wholeness in much the same way. I work with people who have been deeply wounded by trauma. As I assist their bodies in unwinding or releasing the energy of the trauma, it would not be helpful to narrow my awareness to the horror of what's been done to them. Nor would it be helpful if I thought of the trauma as their problem or took it on as my own. What does help is for me to expand my consciousness enough to witness the trauma as connected to all of us. If I can help transform this tiny bit of terror with compassion, we all benefit. If I run from it, or place a boundary between me and what I witness, I add energy to the fear. The cell membrane principles of Oneness and interspace, which I describe in more detail in the next chapter, help me embrace our wholeness and interconnection. At the same time, the principles of containment and selective permeability help me deal with the emotional energy such an experience generates in my healing partners and me.

Collaboration

A small cut in fish flesh made by a sharp rock in the ocean summons a collaborative team of cells into action to do what's necessary to seal the wound and restore equilibrium. When you cut your finger slicing a tomato, the natural healing process is strikingly the same. Both you and the fish come equipped with the same kinds of specialized cells to clot blood, and weave new tissue fibers together while immune cells protect the wounded skin from infection. Health in nature therefore results from a process by which interdependent parts work together to maintain homeostasis or equilibrium. Skillful healing relationships arise out of a sense of partnership with clients, where each of us has a key role to play in determination of the outcome. Likewise, I find increased flexibility and diversity in service to clients when I work with a team of practitioners, each of us acting like specialized cells in cooperation with others.

Homeostasis

Each cell on the planet lives in homeostasis, a biological balancing process, with the cells around it. Illness or symptoms arise in a system out of balance. As cells formed tissues and tissues gathered together to form the organs that eventually became you, the whole process depended on the homeostatic flow of life's juices. The cell membrane is in charge of maintaining homeostatic relationships. Healing relationships benefit from a similar balance of resources and power to sustain health.

Co-evolution

As individuals in a healing relationship, we pay attention to both our internal balance and the effect our individual process is having on those with whom we're in relationship. Everything in nature is connected to everything else in a process of co-evolution; we all evolve together. The oxygen you breathe comes from plants that use the carbon dioxide you exhale. It's a self-organizing process, the origin of which has engaged the mind, heart and spirit of humans over millennia.

Death is not a failure

Death in nature is the beginning of transformation into something else. Dead leaves on the forest floor become the food for not only next year's growth, but also countless numbers of other beings the leaves will become a part of. A great deal of energy is devoted to survival in nature, yet death, rather than being a failure, serves a regenerative function. Spring always follows fall and winter. Real healing relationships can get messy or upsetting and sometimes you might feel like a decomposing leaf with worms eating away at you. Some relationships even need to end for healing to happen. Those we want to help could end up dying. An awareness and acceptance of the natural cycles of light and dark, summer and winter, life and death can prevent fear from stonewalling the relationships we form to support healing. I once worked with a woman with terminal cancer who healed important relationships with her family and came to a sweet and peaceful death once she was able to work through her fear, not of death per se, but of her failure to cure the cancer.

Healing Defined

Taking all these factors into consideration, I've derived the following definition of healing:

> *Healing is the collaborative, transformative process by which balance is restored as we become increas - ingly aware of our wholeness and interconnection with all life.*

Note that I define healing as a *process*, not an act. Certain acts, like surgery, listening and touching may contribute to healing, but these acts are only parts of a bigger process that is ongoing, whether or not we are paying attention. The healing process influences and is influenced by everything else that's going on within and around the individual. To define healing as a process also gets us out of the sticky semantics surrounding the word *healer*. Since healing is a process, a healer becomes simply anyone who facilitates the process. To think of a healer as someone engaged in the act of healing someone implies quite a different power relationship than partners in healing.

The restoration of balance inherent in a healing process manifests on several levels. It could look simply like the restoration of balance in blood sugar, or more complex balance among the physical, emotional, mental and spiritual aspects of our whole being. You may be collaborating with someone to restore balanced functioning within a family or a job environment. Healing happens when balance is restored in the digestive system or in the person's relationship to food or power.

Symptoms let you know when something is off kilter, when you need to pay attention to your healing process. Something hurts or isn't working well in your body. Your job becomes intolerable or you seem to be attracting all the wrong kinds of people and situations in your life. These symptoms may not get your attention right away and they sometimes need to get louder to do so. You tend to say that "something is wrong" when this happens, but actually the body, mind, and spirit are doing just what nature designed them to do. If, on the way to curing symptoms, you become more aware of all that contributes to the symptoms, healing is happening.

I first became aware of the difference between symptom management and a more holistic and interconnected understanding of the healing process in my late thirties. At the time, I was a mother of two children and also running a four-state, citizens' environmental organization. One morning, I was carried out of my house to the hospital on a stretcher with unrelenting back pain. The diagnosis was muscle spasms; the prescription was Valium (a powerful muscle relaxant) and bed rest. Later the doctor recommended a few exercises and milder drugs, but the spasms continued. After months of doing everything the doctor recommended, I was still limited to sitting only 20 minutes at a time, most of the rest of the time lying flat to ease the pain. A friend recommended I see a man who did craniosacral therapy and had helped my friend with his back pain. It sounded pretty strange. I didn't want anyone jerking my vulnerable back around, but by then I would have done just about anything to get out of bed.

6

The gentle hands of Bill, the craniosacral therapist, brought my awareness within, away from family and threatened planet to the mystery of my inner being. As I followed the subtle movement of bones and membranes under his touch, I became increasingly aware of how interconnected my tissues were. I could feel how a subtle shift in my skull bones allowed my spine to find its own balance. A deep level of relaxation that wasn't possible with the drugs accompanied that shift; I learned the difference between numbed and expanded consciousness. The pain gradually reduced and Bill told me that some day I would thank my back for signaling an imbalance that could have lead to more serious problems later in life.

After several sessions with Bill, I was able to move well enough to resume a normal level of activity. I soon learned, however, that there was more going on that couldn't be remedied by these craniosacral adjustments alone. Somehow these sessions with Bill and the slower pace of my life were alerting me to areas of imbalance other than my spinal column. I realized all my energy was going "out there" with nothing left to support my own body. Another friend sent me to LeAnn, who offered family systems therapy. Nothing wrong with my family, I thought! Look how I've been taking care of everyone!

But LeAnn didn't look for what was wrong with my family at all. She merely guided my husband and me through an exploration of the ecology of our families. We looked at patterns and symptoms and how we participated in them. As a biologist and eco-warrior, I was paying attention to the ecological effects of nuclear power, but not to the ecology of my body or family. By only looking outward, I wasn't seeing how the way I was promoting alternative energy ignored the internal power imbalance.

Work with both LeAnn and Bill helped me to restore balance in my body and relationships, while my awareness grew about how everything I did was connected to everything else. I learned that the way I functioned in relationships mattered as much as what I ate. The fear that drove my environmental activism was little different from the fear of loss of power that was driving utilities to use dangerous stuff to fuel our energy habit. As I worked for more balance in all my relationships, my body felt better and I discovered a deeper relationship with Earth, in whose body I was evolving.

Just as my back spasms signaled an imbalance in my life, we also find symptoms of imbalance in communities within Earth. Toxic substances leached from more waste than the Earth can handle show up as illness in plants, animals and humans. Exploitation in all its forms shows up in us as symptoms of imbalance. The increased frequency and intensity of natural disasters tell us the Earth is responding to this imbalance in ways that hurt. We are being asked to wake up, to expand our consciousness to our wholeness and interconnection as part of the global healing process. It can start with your healing relationships.

Note also that this definition of healing states that it is a process by which we become aware of our wholeness and interconnection. It assumes, by nature's standard, that we are already whole and interconnected, which is quite significant. With such a definition, I attest that healing requires a shift of consciousness as much as technological interventions to bring us to the awareness of our interconnection with all life.

The Healing Relationship

A healing relationship is any relationship that facilitates the kind of healing process I just described. More specifically, to meet nature's standard, a relationship is a healing one when all parties are fully engaged a co-creative process, which:

- honors both the integrity of the individual and the relationship they have formed
- fosters trust in themselves, each other and the larger community of life
- helps them expand their consciousness to the interconnection of all life

This may look like a pretty tall order, and you may be thinking that such a relationship is more than you want if you're just trying to help someone feel better. It's certainly possible to be of help

8

to someone without meeting each of these criteria at all times—I certainly don't. We've been trained in models that separate us from nature, the people we're trying to help, and constrict our consciousness of our interconnection with all life. So it may take a while to grow into. I've found that by setting the intention to relate this way, situations appear in just the right time and intensity to take me to the next step on my developmental journey.

A healing relationship doesn't have to be a professional one; you can support healing in any relationship. However, the focus of this book is on the relationship formed between those professionals who want to help and those who come in need of help. I've started to think of those I work with in my practice as *healing partners* rather than clients because it seems to reflect more on the nature of what we're doing. As collaborative partners, the relationship forms the container in which the healing happens.

As you reflect on healing relationships you've had, which ones really made a difference in your overall healing? What made them so? What was missing in the ones in which you weren't helped, or possibly even hurt? In those that were healing, what could you say about the qualities of the relationship that made it so?

When I look back at the relationship with Bill, for example, I remember one session in which he placed his hand very gently on my sternum. It was as though he'd reached deep into my heart to touch a deep well of grief. As I cried, he just held his hand steadily in place, holding the space for me to release the pain. He didn't try to explain it away, or ask me what it meant; he just honored the space I was in, trusting the transformative process in which we were collaboratively engaged. He knew I wouldn't be able to reveal and then release those feelings if I wasn't a full participating partner in the process. He trusted in his own ability to contain whatever feelings my reaction to his touch evoked in him. He also trusted my ability to move through the process and access the support of the larger web of life. We both came to understand that somehow the grief held in my chest was connected to an imbalance in my sacrum as everything shifted after the release.

9

I experienced a healing relationship with LeAnn as well. Her knowledge of how families function as a system was essential to my learning, but I also remember how she would allow the feelings I expressed to settle around me before she offered an explanation. I felt compassion in the space between us when something uncomfortable surfaced between my husband and me. She shared just enough of her own family history to let me know she understood. All families follow these ecological patterns, she said, so that I could better see my own family in a broader context. She respected my knowledge of biology and allowed it to enter her thinking. Years later, when she just happened to move next door to my best friend, we were able to shift roles as we talked over the backyard fence. There was a respect for each other's individual space and an awareness of the bigger relationship field we formed.

LeAnn, Bill and I had each studied the cell membrane years before our meeting, but I don't think we were aware of how the principles by which the cell membrane functions were active as we developed our healing relationships. These are natural principles, after all, and we are natural beings. When you're functioning well in your healing relationships, you're probably following the cell's principles without knowing that's what you're doing.

All relationships that are helpful, however, are not necessarily healing, according to nature's standard. The doctor that delivered my reluctant being into the world with forceps after 27 hours of hard labor probably saved my life, but he was anything but a healer. During several healing encounters over time, I've been able to piece the memory of my birth experience together. I remember how I felt his determined focus on the goal of getting me out, the energy of force, maybe even panic. Not equipped with words or even a brain ready to handle words, I only remember terror in a whole-being neonatal way. Dr. Parsons lacked the knowledge that newborn infants can feel, but my experience with him over the next eight years suggested he couldn't feel either. He treated my various childhood ills, but each encounter was a control battle that neither of us won. Dr. Parsons was never unethical nor did he cross any boundaries; we just never had a healing relationship. That was too bad for both of us.

10

~~~~

The kind of the healing relationship I just defined is fully consistent with an integral model of healing that is currently evolving on the planet. Integral healing sees relationship as the core of healing. It takes us beyond the polarities of technology and heart, mind and body, spirit and science, therapist and client. An integral health paradigm draws upon all of these interdependently to lead to new relationships among the various parts of ourselves, and those with whom we share life on this planet. As the firmly held boundaries between various modalities begin to blur and a more technological approach to healing blends with the heart of the healer, the very basis of our ethical standards is brought into question.

The cell membrane in its elegance, flexibility and sophistication offers a model of relationship practice that takes you beyond the concepts of standard setting, boundaries and legality contained within professional Codes of Ethics to one that aligns your practice with nature's standard. Let's move on, then, to a deeper exploration of the principles by which the cell membrane manages relationships in nature.

Chapter
2

MEET THE CELL MEMBRANE

Imagine yourself at the beginning of your life when you were a single cell. By expanding and contracting in cellular breathing you received nutrients through the membrane that held you together. You were protected and nurtured by a community of cells whose membranes interacted with yours as you were swept along on your way to the safe space that would be your home for nearly nine months. By the time you implanted in your mother's womb, you had divided into two, then four, then many cells. As your cells divided, the membrane surrounding each one managed the new relationships being formed among these cells and all those that surrounded them. Your cells differentiated into various forms and functions through the collaboration of the membrane with the DNA blueprint in the center of each cell to finally become the complex, highly conscious being you are. You are still imbedded in a community of life whose relationships are managed by cell membranes.

Your healing relationships can evolve just as you have evolved—with the cell membrane guiding the way. With the cell membrane as a model, your healing relationships can become the safe space in which you and your healing partners differentiate and heal in the growing awareness of your interconnection with all life.

I knew about the cell membrane when I started my first job as a social worker, but I didn't know its principles were active as I formed relationships with my patients and their families in a physical rehabilitation hospital. Every patient there was trying to adapt to life after a traumatic change in their body: stroke, spinal cord or head injury, amputation, etc. That first year was really rough—one in which everything I learned about boundaries and professional demeanor in graduate school was challenged. These patients and their loved ones wouldn't let me retreat behind a professional screen, but drew me into the realization that *healing is a co-creative process.*

In this new setting, I encountered women in the prime of life struck down by stroke, unable to speak or comb their own hair, athletes unable to walk, and children who couldn't open their eyes. As I watched people not be able to reach their mouth with a spoon, dribbling noodles down their bibs, I felt really uncomfortable. I tried hard to create a boundary between us—one that would protect me from feeling like them. On the outside I looked calm and professional, but inside the fear of disability for my loved ones and myself kept pushing against that boundary. It was tough to feel separate when some of the women triggered memories of my grandmother staring blankly at her dinner plate and drooling. I squirmed inside, knots formed in my gut and I found myself detouring around the hospital dining area so I wouldn't have to see them. I noticed how hardened some of the veteran staff had become, walling themselves off from the suffering of others. Then there were others without any boundary at all who took all the suffering into their own bodies on the way to a quick burnout. I didn't want to either harden or become a sopping emotional rag. What I had learned in graduate school about keeping a professional boundary, a sense of being separate while still showing unconditional regard now seemed so abstract and unreal. I felt cast adrift without a compass in the healing relationship sea. Upon reflection, I think the formulation of the cell membrane as that compass began then. Let me tell you about one case in particular that helped me discover what I now understand as the cell membrane's lessons for the helping professional.

I was assigned to work with a 15-year-old boy, Richard, who was in a coma from a traumatic head injury. He arrived at the unit dressed in a t-shirt covered with a picture of a largemouth bass rising to snatch the bait. My 15-year-old son had a shirt just like it. Both boys had dark curly hair and large eyes. Richard, however, lay silent in his room, unresponsive to any attempts to stimulate him into consciousness. I worked with his mother, listening to her, helping her with insurance and educational forms, but I avoided direct contact with Richard. I just couldn't. I told myself there really wasn't much I could do to help this comatose boy anyway. Social workers talked to patients, and this boy not only couldn't talk, but we had no idea if he could even hear. Bringing Richard back to consciousness wasn't in my job description. If he woke up, I'd talk to him then, I told myself. As I passed his room, I could almost feel parts of me closing off—avoiding the fear that asked for attention.

One day, as I dashed past the physical therapy gym, the physical therapist working with Richard called me for help. She needed someone to hold his head while she manipulated another part of his body. "Oh, boy," I thought, "here I go – I've got to touch him. No way out of this!" Supporting his head in my arm, as I once did with my son, I just listened to Richard's breathing which drew me deeper inside his being. "Someone is in there! I can feel him!" No, he wasn't talking or even blinking, but I could feel his essence as clearly as I feel my son's. What convinced me that what I was feeling was real, and not just my projection of something I wanted to feel, was that the essence of Richard had its own unique quality, a quality very different from my son's, in fact different from anyone else's I had ever met. It wasn't just that he was still alive, but that the quality of his energy was uniquely Richard and not somebody else. It's like when you hold a newborn infant; even though he can't talk or respond you can connect with his unique being. Richard felt like *his* mother's son, not mine.

It was the first time I ever encountered what felt like consciousness unlimited by the brain or physical structure, yet encompassing it somehow. The physical therapist sensed it, too, and we wondered about it as we visited later. Around that same time quite a few scientists were awakening to this reality, but we wouldn't learn about that research for a few years. In his book, *The Mystery of Mind*, neurosurgeon Wilder Penfield, concluded that consciousness does not have its source in the brain. Since then many other scientists have reached the same conclusion. After a lifetime of study in physics and things tangible, astronaut Edgar Mitchell awakened to a consciousness beyond, yet encompassing physical form as he viewed the Earth from space. It changed his life, as my encounter with Richard changed mine. There were no words exchanged between Richard and me, no specific messages except a powerful and clear feeling of intimacy. His presence impacted my life and my presence impacted his. Richard was no longer just an inert body to be moved by a therapist, but someone the PT and I held in awareness of a consciousness that survives severe brain injury.

As I reflect on my work with Richard and his family, I realize how the principles by which the cell membrane of all living things manages relationships were at work then in my relationships with them. The underlying assumptions of what I was taught about the therapeutic relationship and professional ethics expands when looked at through the cell membrane model. Other stories of relationships with colleagues and patients in that setting emerge now as I reflect on those early attempts to develop healing relationships. Let's look at each of these cell membrane principles, one by one, to see how they were active as I discovered the co-creative potential in healing relationships. As you read my stories, I invite you into some of your own, where the cell membrane was a silent partner in your healing.

CONTAINMENT

If we look at cells under a microscope, the first thing we notice about the membrane surrounding each cell is that it holds the cell together; it contains it. Without it there'd be a mass of confusion—protoplasm flowing mindlessly everywhere, never getting any work done. That would be like you running around trying to help someone without being pulled together inside your skin. The membrane is not solid, like a boundary or wall, but a fluid, crystalline matrix that shifts and changes somewhat depending on the work the cell is doing in relation to all other cells. It's made in two layers of molecules, each layer accepting one kind of substance and not another. It's similar to the mental and emotional filters through which you receive or reject certain kinds of information. The membrane still retains its identity, its overall shape and function as it shifts in response to what's happening around it. Likewise, you can hold your identity, emotions and skills inside your individual container, but be ready to respond to what's needed by your healing partner.

Richard, the boy in a coma, and I, his social worker, are contained in our individual bodies, each wrapped in our own skin. Just as you can tell a heart cell from a lung cell by its form and what it's outer membrane looks like, Richard and I are clearly separate beings with our own shape, history, emotions and mission in life. We're held together, like cells, in individual packages surrounded by our skin (like the cell membrane) through which we send and receive signals from our environment. We have access to each other, in part, by our skin. Openings in our skin, like our eyes, nose, ears, anus, etc. are

16

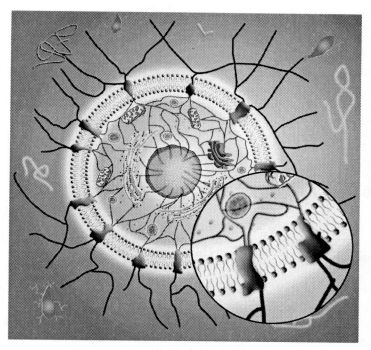

Figure 1. The Living Cell with it's membrane magnified

specialized and selective to take in what our bodies need and release what we don't. Because our skin and its organs are composed of cells that follow certain principles in deciding what goes out and comes in, our whole body follows those same principles. Once nature finds a pattern that works, it gets repeated at each level of being.

But there's more to the containers of Richard and Diane than meets the eye. An invisible (to all but clairvoyant people and specialized photographic equipment) field of energy surrounds and interpenetrates our body that also contains us. It contains energetic patterns that define us, hold our history and serve as a container with which we interact with those around us on a more subtle level than our skin. These energetic patterns still honor the same principles as the skin and cell membrane. When I held Richard's head, while the PT worked his legs, the nonphysical containers around and within our bodies began to communicate with each other and it seemed like we all felt it—even the boy with the severely damaged brain.

While Richard never awakened from his coma, there was another boy, Brian, who did. After Brian woke up, he told me, by pointing to letters on a spelling board, how he perceived what was happening in his parents' relationship during the time he was in a coma and just before he came out of it. In fact, that's why he woke up—he was concerned about his parents. These and other patients helped me become aware of this energetic container long before I studied energy healing. It not only contains us, but serves as the energetic field through which both conscious and unconscious communication occurs, which I'll get into in more detail later.

The principle of containment is the closest thing in nature to our idea of a boundary in relationships, but expands it in a more interactive way. It's like a boundary in that you live in your space and I in mine, you have your feelings and personal process and I have mine, but containment recognizes both separateness *and* interconnectedness. In healing relationships, you honor your own container and that of your client's in many ways, just like when you set a boundary. With Richard, when our staff did what we could to keep him safe, clean and nurtured, we were honoring the principle of containment. Containment was at work also when we took care of our own bodies by using good body mechanics as we lifted him. We contained our feelings of fear or helplessness as we touched and watched his inert form. However, as I describe the other principles, you'll see how the cell membrane provides flexibility as well as protection between you and your healing partner. But first, let's look a little further into how the principle of containment facilitates healing.

Containment vs. suppression

My work with Richard began to teach me the difference between containment and suppression, as well. I had been suppressing my fears of a similar trauma happening to my son when I walked past his room without looking in. I didn't want to deal with the fear, so I

18

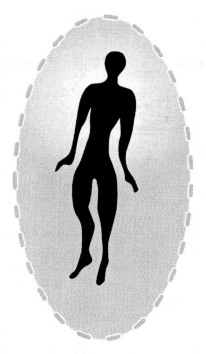

Figure 2. Containment: Individual
Personal Space

ended up distancing myself from Richard. But in the presence of
Richard's spirit, I couldn't do that for long. In the peacefulness
revealed from within his damaged body, my fear both surfaced and
softened somehow. By containing and not suppressing the fear, it
was more accessible to me. Richard wasn't taking care of me, but
when I was with him, in some mysterious way, I was able to look at
my fear within a different context. Of course, I still feared something
like that could happen to my son, but I had a little more trust that if
it did, I'd be better prepared. If I had continued to suppress the fear,
it would have gotten stronger and Richard wouldn't have had the
benefit of my presence. Suppression keeps our feelings out of view.
Containment holds them in awareness until we can work to accept
and transform them.

Create a safe space for your healing partner's feelings.

If I had told Richard's mother, Julia, how much I was afraid that the same thing would happen to my son, I wouldn't be honoring the principle of containment. By not containing my feelings, I'd flood her with them—which she certainly didn't need. In her grief and despair, she said things like, "no one understands what this is like for me." I helped her contain her feelings by just reflecting back to her, "Yes, I probably don't. Can you tell me what it's like?" If I couldn't contain my own fears of being in her situation, I couldn't create the space for her to express hers, or my well-chosen words would carry the energy of my fear.

Most professional standards of practice align themselves well with the principle of containment by placing a lot of importance on client confidentiality. The client's experience is his own. Whatever goes on in his body, mind or heart is his to share with others—or not—and we must ask his permission before we share it with anyone else, even when we think it's for his own benefit. The principle of containment allows for the information to stay within the relationship where it can be most beneficial for the person's healing.

Containment allows healing to happen where and in whom it's needed.

If you take a client's pain or joy (or other feelings) into your own personal space, you deprive them of the opportunity to be fully aware of and responsive to what's happening inside their personal container. If you take on responsibility for what a client is experiencing, they cannot fully experience it and feel the empowerment that results when something is resolved. For example, when Julia had an emotional meltdown in my office, if I had moved into her personal space and feelings, wrapped her with a big hug, saying "Now, now, it'll be okay, " I would have moved into her container and smothered her. I might have even filled her space with my need to fix her or take over her burden. Such a reaction could stifle her expression, not just contain it. Imagine if instead I just softened a little in my own body and maybe allowed my arms and chest to open slightly—just enough to hold the space for the intense feelings she was expressing. Only the compassion in my heart would be flooding her grief and despair. Once contained, the potency of the feeling and the compassionate energy of the therapist could facilitate both a release and a transformation of the grief and despair.

Containment adds potency to the healing process.

One day, Richard's mom became angry in a conference with the doctor and yelled, "What? You want to put Richard through one more *&$%!# test? How much more do you need to know! He's in a coma, damn it! I guess it keeps money flowing into your coffers, doesn't it?" Our compassionate physician heard her anger and also sensed the deeper pain under it. He didn't consciously know the cell membrane principle of containment was at work when he tried to support her, but when he said, "It does seem like a lot of testing, doesn't it, and it's probably hard to see the value in it," he was helping her contain the feeling. "Hell, yes!" she shouted, "Poor baby probably feels like a pin cushion.....if he could feel.....that is...." and she broke into tears. Rather than justifying more tests, which would have just fueled another angry reaction, Dr. R. simply let her know he heard her feelings, and affirmed them. In this way he helped her go deeper into the potency of the anger to reach and eventually release the sadness. In the presence of that kind of support, Julia could not only better engage in collaborative treatment planning with Dr. R., but heal through her emotions too.

As Dr R. was able to meet Julia in her helplessness, he also became aware of his own helplessness in the situation. Not seeing any improvement in Richard's condition, he hadn't realized how much his sense of powerlessness had caused him to reach for the diagnostic manual. By not taking on or reacting to Julia's anger, he was better able to discover and be with his own powerless feelings— a pretty potent experience for those dedicated to healing. It was his 6th encounter this week with a seemingly hopeless situation, so the encounter with Julia helped him learn nature's lesson, that sometimes there really isn't anything you can do but be compassionate.

If the doctor had thrown up the boundary of his being the one in charge of the treatment plan, the one who ought to know and the family as the ones who needed him to know, the potency of healing in this case would be diminished. Containment helped it be a more healing exchange which built a safer relationship container for the more difficult decisions that lay ahead for Richard's healing team, of which his mother was a central member. Containment, along with the other principles of the cell membrane model, takes ethics a little beyond informed consent as just an exchange of information between separate individuals to a more natural collaborative process.

A subtle difference exists in the consciousness that arises around the sense of a membrane that contains and a boundary that divides. If you imagine a flexible, responsive membrane, it looks quite different from a rigid territorial boundary that requires more effort to both sustain and tear down. If you, as a helper, are aware that such a membrane holds you and your partner together, you may find that you can feel safe inside your own physical and energetic skin, yet still connected with each other. Let's look now at another way nature offers us this model of greater flexibility and selectivity in how we relate, moment-by-moment, to our healing partners.

Chapter 4

SELECTIVE PERMEABILITY

Selective permeability refers to the discerning process by which both cells and people relate to one another. Cell membranes are equipped with special molecules called receptors that vibrate at a certain frequency to attract only those messages that fit its frequency. Messages from one cell reach a receptor in another, and they ring each other's bell. The communication process in both cell membranes and healing relationships is based on *resonance*—a match in vibrational frequency between something ready to respond and the vibration which triggers the response. Whether we're referring to an electron ready to jump into a higher orbit in an atom, or a client wanting to jump into your arms, resonance refers to just the right fit between the message being sent and a receptor ready to take it in. When the student is ready, the teacher will come.

In the personal energy field and the field of the relationship we don't actually have receptors that look and function exactly like those on the cell membrane. When I say receptors resonate with each other in a relationship, I'm referring to structures of consciousness, those invisible energetic patterns that resonate with those of others in relationship. The receptors activated in a relationship are not the actual receptors on our cell membranes, but the beliefs, thoughts and emotions that resonate with those on the same wavelength in our partner. Even though what happens in the relationship field can actually influence what happens on our physical cell membrane receptors, and thus our biology, the receptors I talk about here exist in the non-physical realm of consciousness. In my practice I've discovered that these consciousness receptors follow principles similar to those of the physical receptors.

When separate sound waves, like from two or more tuning forks come into resonance, the sound is amplified. When something in your healing partner resonates in you, you'll each become more aware of what you may not have "heard" before.

Dr. R and Richard's mother, in their interaction around further diagnostic testing for Richard, resonated with each other around their helplessness with his coma. Richard's unresponsiveness pushed both of their helplessness buttons, you might say, which became more apparent to them in their exchange. If Julia hadn't blown up at his suggestion for more tests, he may not have been aware that his helplessness was behind his order for the tests. Containment helped both of them become more aware of which receptors were active and reach a more collaborative and healing response to the situation.

When our healing partners push our buttons, it lets us know which receptors are being activated by the relationship. Richard's condition certainly pushed my mother fear buttons. The middle-aged women with strokes triggered yet another kind of fear receptor for me. All these triggers tell us that something in one person resonates in another, activating receptors in each partner.

Richard's mom and I both had a set of receptors that resonated with similar sets of receptors in most mothers. Mothers of all cultures and time are hard-wired with receptors that respond to their children's cries, their need for food or a soothing touch. Yet each of our receptors was shaped differently by *how* we were mothered, by how our mother responded to our cry or how she touched us. I never learned how Julia was mothered, but as a single mom with a younger daughter, her mothering receptors were influenced by her lack of support from the children's father and mounting medical bills. She was overwhelmed by grief and so much to take care of. Her receptors were ringing, and as you'll see, mine had been conditioned over at least three generations of mothers to answer her call.

My receptors were colored by the fact that my great-grand-mother died when my grandmother was just six, leaving her to care for her three younger brothers. Many years later, Baba, as I called my grandmother, found her 2 year-old daughter drowned in their duck pond. My grandfather was advised by their doctor to get Baba pregnant again as the best cure for her unrelenting grief, and my mother was conceived. Mom's developing prenatal receptors, there-fore, were bathed in Baba's grief and her father's intention that little Ann (my Mom) take care of it for her. Two years later, Mom's father died suddenly, leaving Baba with 6 children to care for and no time for her grief, yet again.

Emotional energetic patterns influence the development of family receptors through the generations. The three-generational pattern would have been enough to give me a pretty sensitive set of maternal receptors around loss and taking responsibility for anoth-er's grief, but I got another shot of it in the womb. I was conceived to keep my father out of World War II, as I learned later when I asked

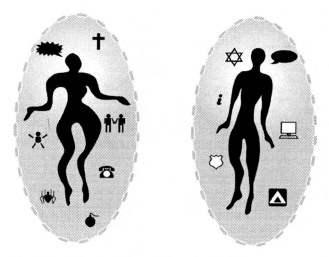

Figure 3. Selective Permeability: Symbols for specific receptors contained within the personal field of two indi-viduals, e.g. communication style, religion, relation-ships, etc.

why my father's buddies jokingly called me Dad's "draft defer-ment." I failed in that, however, so when I was just a few months old my father left for Europe, not to return until I was nearly three. So by the time I encountered Julia in her deep need to be taken care of in her grief, I had a pretty finely tuned set of receptors ready to answer the call of her *grief* and *take-care-of-me* receptors. Of course, the transmission of family traits is a more complex process than I've outlined here, but can't you just hear the resonance between Julia and me? Our receptors and the vibrational messages we sent to each other fit like a lock and key, just like the molecular receptors on the cells of your body. Add that to my fear that it could be my son lying there in a coma, and the potential for emotional enmeshment—drowning in each other's emotional waters—was pretty great. So was the potential for healing—for both of us.

Resonance and selectivity

The potential for healing arises from the interaction of resonance and selectivity. Let me explain. Instead of a boundary that suggests totally separate emotional and psychological processes in each per-son, selective permeability acknowledges the power of resonance in relationships. You can't help but affect and be affected by those you meet in your practice, yet selective permeability informs you further that you can make conscious choices, much in the way a cell does, about what you express in the relationship space you share with oth-ers. Julia's *need-for-help* receptors activated my *need-to-help* recep-tors. If I was aware that I was feeling the need to help, I could have chosen, according to selective permeability, how to respond. In the best-case scenario, I would notice, "Oh, there it is again! I want to rush over and take care of her so she doesn't hurt anymore." I could then contain those feelings within my own emotional field with a promise to support myself later, and choose to not take Julia's feel-ings into my personal space. I would also consciously choose to send only compassionate messages to Julia, not the energy of my need to help. In a space free of my needs, Julia's helpless receptors would be bathed only in compassion.

26

As a beginning social worker, however, without the conscious knowledge of a cell membrane model to guide me in these situations, I wasn't always conscious of what receptors were active in me; nor was I able to choose the most compassionate response. I thought I had to maintain my protective boundaries, keep that wall between Julia's pain and what it might touch in me. In thinking there was a boundary, I unconsciously over-functioned in the relationship with Julia, really believing my inner process wasn't influencing how I responded to her. At times, however, those *need-to-help* receptors, and difficulty with the grief of others kept talking to me after I got home. I'd feel edgy and emotional. By consulting with my supervisor, I was able to find support for these painful feelings and understand them better. Once I attended to my own helplessness and grief, I noticed I was less reactive with Julia. I realize now, I was becoming friendlier with my own receptors; I knew I couldn't leave my feelings at the door. I learned how, by being compassionate with my own inner doubts and fears, to create a compassionate, and not emotionally muddied, space for my clients.

It takes practice to become more conscious of what your clients activate in your own receptors and make healing choices in your response. Remember, healing partnerships in which both parties can grow and heal is nature's way. Even though your partner's healing is in the foreground of the relationship, you can get your daily consciousness exercise just by going to work and attending to what comes forward. Chapter 9 outlines a process that can help you get your exercise in and out of sessions. But first there's more about selective permeability that can feed your growing awareness.

Receptors grow, change and evolve throughout life.

Receptors are not fixed at birth, but shift and change in response to what's happening around them. If I had met Julia's grief receptors with my family's grief energy, her grief receptors would have been re-energized. In other words, if healing partners just flood each other's receptors with the same emotional energy they're already resonating with, the lifelong patterns get reinforced and will contin-

27

ue to attract similar emotional experiences in relationships. If, however, those painful feelings in the client are met with compassion by a therapist who has learned to contain and work with her own pain, something new happens. Instead of the client's receptors being bathed in the therapist's anxiety, they are bathed in her compassion, which helps them heal. As Marc Ian Barasch says in his book, *Field Notes on the Compassionate Life*, "Compassion isn't simply opening a spigot and coating everything in a treacly, all-purpose goo." I experience compassion as an ability to stand in the presence of suffering, to be with the suffering of another in the full awareness that we are interconnected. It's different from pity, in that I'm not feeling something for another, but standing in the presence of something all humans share. Compassion isn't a technique, but something that arises from the heart, grounded in the awareness of interconnection.

In Julia's case, for example, if her grief receptors were initially tuned by loss that was either not acknowledged, or maybe even belittled, a new experience with compassion can help them shift and grow. They might now hum a slightly different tune. Receptors respond to changes in their environment, whether that change is helpful or not. We, as health professionals, will affect the quality of the environment that bathes our partner's receptors, so it's a good thing we can grow in our ability to make choices in how we respond. Each time we respond compassionately, to our own feelings and others, our receptors grow in their capacity for compassion.

Transference, counter transference and projection

Another way to look at the receptor resonance process is to view receptors as magnets and targets for the transference, counter transference and projection processes that take place in healing relationships. In transference your partner transfers their need for the ideal parent, lover or healer to you. In counter transference, you respond according to your need to be that ideal. In the natural process of projection, we tend to think that what we're feeling came from our partner or we project our own uncomfortable feelings onto our partner. In all three of these processes, messages are being sent back and forth between resonating receptors. For example, Julia's needs served as the magnet for my need to help; my need to help found a target in Julia. There needs to be a fit between receptors in order for projection to happen. Without my need-to-help someone in grief receptors, Julia's grief wouldn't be able to find such a good fit in my receptor field; the resonance would have been different. If I had healed my *need-to-help* receptors before meeting her, that healing process would have helped me recognize her grief, but not be reactive to it out of my own unresolved needs.

It's not that projection or transference is harmful; in fact, both are quite natural. It's the way nature, and our nervous system, awakens us to how we perceive what's around us. Selective permeability, however, invites us to make conscious choices once we get the message.

Selective permeability informs us further that what we're feeling in the moment depends on the configuration of our receptors *and* the quality of the message sent by the partner. *Both partners are responsible for the relationship exchange*, whether you're involved in projection or transference dynamics. This is key, because it's important to realize that something in you is serving as the magnet for that projection or transference. Your parenting receptors can be a magnet for your partner's need for an ideal parent. Likewise, your partner's needs for an ideal parent can attract either your need to parent, an aversion to parenting or your compassionate parent messengers, depending on where you are in your parenting development.

Your partner's receptors can attract whatever you're not comfortable with and make it more known to you. For example, I sometimes attract situations with my partners that force me to take notice of my *competence* receptors. When I react to a partner's claim that I'm the healer that saved their life, or they express their disappointment that nothing is improving, selective permeability tells me that transference is happening and both of us have activated receptors that need to be attended to. I'm not talking about the genuine and important exchanges of gratitude that occur in healing relationships, or even the valuable assessment of what's working and what isn't in a healing process. What I'm talking about here is what happens in my competency receptor when someone attributes great healing powers—or disappointment—to me. If I'm having trouble acknowledging and accepting my skills, or fear that I'm not very competent at all, these attributions can awaken those concerns. Likewise, if my partner has trouble validating her own role in healing, she would attribute anything that happens in the session to me. In such a situation, we both have active receptors to look at. If I notice and contain my own reactivity, I'm better able to help her contain her own feelings in a way that empowers her.

That changes the level of responsibility for what's happening a little, doesn't it? When Julia was projecting her anger and frustration at Dr. R, he didn't just lob it back to her, thinking it was her problem. His helplessness, which was awakened in their exchange, played a role in the transmission. Something about him made it safe for Julia to send the anger message around her helplessness or maybe just provide a strong magnet to draw it out of her. Their receptors were in cahoots, so to speak, to enable both of them to pay attention to their inner process. I don't mean to imply that our healing partners are there for our healing, but just that we each carry responsibility for the resonance between us.

The fact that membranes are selectively permeable represents only part of the reason the cell membrane principles provide growth and health enhancing qualities to your relationships. The principle I call "interspace" expands our understanding of the healing relationship even further.

Chapter
5

INTERSPACE

Cells live in a sea of fluid that carries the vital molecules and energy they draw upon to nurture, communicate and heal. That medium, called interstitial fluid, bathes all cells in one organ or body, and also connects that body, through breath, food and energy, with all other forms of life. Except in the rare but important functions of defense and sex, cells don't interact by interpenetrating one another. All other interactions take place in the interstitial fluid, as receptors on the cell membrane select what to draw from the fluid. Cells decide what to excrete through their membranes into the fluid to support the life of the whole body and the whole body of Earth.

I call the medium that carries messages from one human being to another in relationship "interspace." Interspace functions like the interstitial fluid that flows around all cells; it's the medium through which you send messages back and forth with your healing partners. The messages can be physical, through touch and manipulation, verbal or energetic. Richard and I continued throughout his stay in the hospital to relate to each other through what I now understand as interspace. I sat at his bedside, sometimes held his hand, and just connected. We were simply present to each other—"hooked up"—as Milton Trager, the creator of Trager massage calls it.

When you talk with someone on the telephone, you know the difference if you're talking to someone dear to you, than, say, to a telemarketer. The phone is the same, the sounds are transmitted through the same telephone lines or wireless towers, yet, because of

the thoughts, feelings and intentions you each contribute to the relationship space you form together, both participants can sense the difference in the quality of the relationship. You may have even noticed
that when someone very close to you calls you know who it is before
you pick up the phone. Interspace changes as the relationship
changes. If you think now of someone you talked to yesterday, you
probably can still tap into the quality of that energetic highway
between you.

As health practitioners, we carry the responsibility to hold
interspace in our awareness and keep it safe. Interspace is the con-

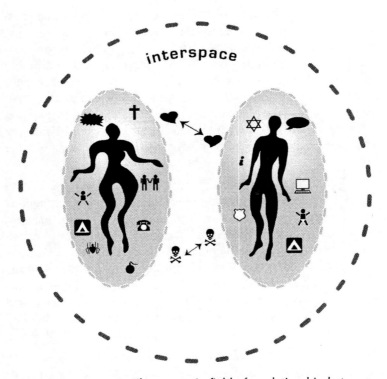

Figure 4. Interspace: The energetic field of a relationship between
two people showing receptor resonance in the areas of love and a
sense of danger.

tainer of the healing relationship, which requires as much attention as the individual personal space of each partner. Because each healing partner has the power to influence change in the other, it's important to consciously place in interspace only those thoughts and feelings that serve the wellbeing of our partner. For example, when I became aware of how much fear I felt when I looked at Julia's son, it would not have served her healing if I had chosen to tell her that. I would have been flavoring the interspace with my fear, adding more fear to bathe her fear receptors. With Julia, I chose to send messages of compassion and caring into interspace, while containing the fear. Our mother receptors were in resonance, but I had the responsibility to the healing relationship to choose whether it would be my *fearful mother* or *compassionate* mother receptors that sent messages into interspace.

The quality of the relationship space Julia and I created with each other affected not only Richard but also other members of our rehab team and the hospital at large. When two cells or organs in a body are working well together, the fluid that flows to all the other tissues is healthier. In a holistic system, the thoughts, feelings and intentions of each part of the system contribute to the flavor of the juices that flow around and through all of them. It's like the way all the vegetables in soup both flavor and are flavored by the broth. If you're standing in a room with a few people having a good time and someone enters the room looking angry or menacing, you'll all feel it, even if nothing is said or no one is touched. When this happens, you're responding to what's been placed in interspace by all of you, which shifted when the new person entered. Each member of the original group will respond to the menacing presence of the new person according to the conditioning of their own receptors, but everyone will be touched, nevertheless.

As my skills for creating and holding healing relationships grew, so also did my appreciation of the power of interspace. I work more intentionally with interspace now, over 20 years since I experienced it with Richard and his mom. I often allow time for what's said to hang in interspace before responding. The thoughts, feelings and intentions of the words we put there have a way of interacting and then touching each of us in creative ways, just like the molecules that float around each cell in your body. I take time before, during and after a therapeutic session to notice what's happening in interspace, to taste the flavor of the broth, so to speak. When I work with couples, I direct their attention to what is active in each of them in response to something, but also bring their attention to how their words and actions are affecting the relationship space they share. It helps them experience the effect of their individual process on the relationship they say they want to nurture, but often pollute with their uncontained reactivity. I'm always impressed by what happens when they bring their attention consciously to interspace. The anger, hurt or betrayal they dumped there undergoes a kind of alchemical transformation when just held in awareness. Soon something shifts and the couple experiences something new. This kind of shift leads us to another cell membrane principle—differentiation.

DIFFERENTIATION

Differentiation is a key force in the ongoing process of evolution on the planet. Plants and animals, after a period of being quite set in their niche in life, grow new receptors or modify old ones whenever they have to adapt to changes in their environment. As external conditions keep pressing upon them, they gradually change into organisms that look significantly different from their ancestors. Nerve cords evolved into complex central nervous systems and eventually into our big highly differentiated brain. Individuals in healing relationships evolve too, and it is this differentiating quality that allows for greater flexibility as we respond to challenging situations with our partners. I first observed this as the various therapeutic disciplines in the rehabilitation hospital were asked to differentiate.

Back in the 1980s, rehabilitation hospitals were among the first to develop interdisciplinary teams, and we worked hard to make ours work for the benefit of our patients. Fresh out of a graduate program that cultivated an ecological perspective on human behavior, I was eager to participate in this creative team program. Our director kept emphasizing the difference between multidisciplinary (where several specialists worked with the same patient) and interdisciplinary teams. The latter implied that the team—which consisted of at least a doctor, nurse, physical, occupational, recreational and speech therapists, and social worker—coordinate our work together such that our treatment program was both integrative and fit the specific needs of the patient and his family. In other words, the boundaries between individual modalities were beginning to fall away back then, and nature's more collaborative approach to healing was evolving among health practitioners.

For veteran therapists this new arrangement was quite a challenge. Just like stomach cells that evolved to excrete digestive juices, our therapists were used to well-defined tasks, based on their respective training. Stomach cells eventually differentiated, however, to include emotional sensation (among other things) in their job description, and evolved new receptors to do so. Stomach cells began to share function and communicate intimately with the nerve and endocrine cells to maintain homeostasis within the whole organism. In order to function as an interdisciplinary team, we were all asked to differentiate, to expand our understanding of our jobs to collaborate more like cells in nature.

All professional codes of ethics direct you to work only within the scope of practice for which you've been trained. Nurses don't prescribe drugs, occupational therapists don't treat bedsores, and social workers don't hold heads in physical therapy sessions. We work only with the receptors we've developed in our training, right? Yes, our team agreed, but the differentiation principle had something more to teach us about scope of practice. One day a young female physical therapist came to my office asking to talk about a problem. She reported that one of the young patients on our unit wanted to talk to her about his fears regarding loss of sexual function because of his spinal cord injury. She was close to his age, and a very compassionate and wise woman with whom he probably felt very safe asking about these things. It wasn't the first time a young man had reached out to her in this way; she seemed to have the receptor for it—or at least one ready to develop.

Dealing with sexuality was a job shared by the physician and me, but she was the one with whom his receptors were buzzing. She felt she needed permission to go beyond the boundaries of her profession to just be a good listener and maybe offer some information that may help him understand the sexual options now available to him. I inquired a little about her feelings for the young man and then gave her some information about sexuality after spinal cord injury. I trusted that she knew how to respond to transference and that with this information she may be able to help the young man find greater motivation for relearning to walk. Like the stomach cell doing both digestion and sensation, she was differentiating to help him in more ways than ambulation training. Not only did she help this young man, but now she was better able to help subsequent patients as well. She had evolved, just as cell membranes evolve, to expand her capacity to facilitate healing. In this way the cell membrane model supports both responsible scope of practice and growth.

Our team grew as an ecosystem grows. We each did our respective jobs based on our training, but our patients and the power of differentiation also stretched us to grow new receptors to respond to patients' needs. Sometimes my job became one of supporting other therapists as they moved into new territory with patients. In our team meetings with the patient and family, I often watched in wonder as Dr. R discussed psychosocial issues and I was the one talking about the justification for six more weeks of speech therapy. I'll never forget the day when Matt, a head-injured family man left our unit able to live a full and rich life. He seemed transformed into a much more pleasant guy than the angry drunk who sent his head through the windshield of his truck. Our team gathered around him and his family in the knowledge that all of us grew a little and differentiated in the four months he was on our unit. None of us were the same as we continued to let other patients shape our receptors as we all evolved.

That rehab team laid the ground for me to continue to differentiate my healing gifts, such as learning energy healing. My role in healing relationships differentiates as healing partners challenge me to draw upon qualities within that are ready to evolve, new receptors ready to unfold. They help me discover another principle at work in cell membranes and healing relationships: the importance of being able to connect with the Center of my being, the place that knows my evolutionary journey and the decisions that will keep me on the path.

Chapter
7

CONNECT TO CENTER

All tempest has,
like a navel,
a hole in its middle, through which
a gull can fly
in silence

14th Century Japanese, anonymous

Confusion, self-doubt, and competing thoughts sometimes whirl like a tempest within as we engage in healing relationships. Do you sometimes long for a place to go, a place where the answer to the confusion awaits you like the silent place that calls to the gull? Cell membranes have such a place to connect to, a place that contains the full complement of the organism's potential and the part each cell plays in reaching that potential. It's called the genetic code, or DNA, which lives within the nucleus, the cell's center. The cell membrane and nucleus "talk" to each other all the time. The membrane lets the nucleus know, in its vibrational and chemical language, what's happening in the whirl of information around the cell, and the nucleus responds by uncovering and unwinding just the right section of the code to build a molecule that meets the need of that cell in relation to the whole organism. Neither the membrane nor the nucleus of the cell acts alone, but in intimate relationship.

Differentiation and centering work hand in hand. When my receptors started itching to grow in directions other than my usual scope of practice, something in my Center started giving me instructions on what was needed next. At first, I didn't listen to that little voice inside that said, "You're ready to play a different role in healing. Your energy is being drained by ordering wheelchairs and walkers for patients, when it's your touch they need." "Oh, no, that's too risky," I retorted. "Energy work is weird; social work is safe. I get a regular paycheck; people like and respect me here. I can't throw all that away!" So in the whirl of messages, I got sick—really sick. I had pneumonia for five weeks and couldn't get out of bed without help. I had plenty of time to listen to my inner guide then. It was so hard to consider resigning from the hospital, not knowing how I would pay my bills or where I would go to find the sense of community I enjoyed at the hospital. But every time I connected to my Center, the message was the same, "Time to move on." Two weeks after resigning, I was offered an adjunct teaching position in the social work school from which I'd graduated. It offered not only another differentiating opportunity (I had never taught before) but also just the right amount of money for rent to support my budding private practice.

From the cell membrane perspective, my receptors were detecting a less than healthy fit between my growing skills and the hospital environment in which I worked. They let my Center know it was time to start turning out messages that would help me reach my growth potential

How do you tap into the wisdom within? How do you experience your Center—the safe place that offers a calm refuge and guidance in times of difficulty in your work? We all have different ways of finding our center, and Chapter 9 offers suggestions on how to do that, but the important thing is knowing it's there, ready to guide you when you need it. I find I have different kinds of centers, or maybe tap into different dimensions within when I need help in sessions: body alignment, breath, my inner wisdom or the healing contract. All of them contribute to the center with a capital "C"—the Center that guides the most healing response from the healer within.

Alice comes to mind as a client who taught me the most about following guidance from Center. She challenged me to use all the principles I'm writing about in this book, but it was Centering that was the most operative one at the crucial moments. Alice, a woman in her seventies, lived her life in perpetual depression, along with all the bodily dysfunction asociated with that. You name it and she had it. After months of working with her, I was ready to throw in the towel; we were wasting Medicare's money. No matter what we did, Alice stayed as depressed and in pain as ever, even as she was getting every medication known to science to combat both. She found some comfort in the imagery work we were doing together, but insisted that the calm never lasted much past the time I got out the door.

One day, I was running errands in the neighborhood where Alice was living in a nursing facility. It was Saturday I remember, my day off, but something inside told me to go see Alice. I didn't trust intuitive hunches much in those days, didn't recognize it as a voice from Center. My rational mind couldn't just let me respond to intuition, so I reasoned that I could save gas and time by going today while I was in the neighborhood instead of Tuesday, our next scheduled appointment. It was a beautiful late winter Kansas day, when hints of green and a change in light tease you into thinking spring is near. I remember the shade of green peeking out in tiny buds on trees against the clear blue sky as I rounded the corner to the nursing home. Inside, a flutter of anticipation, quite uncharacteristic of my usual approach to a visit with Alice, wouldn't be denied. I thought she might have died! Those messages from Center aren't always clear, you know.

"Hello! I knew you'd come," she said as I entered the room. "Can you see it? The pink?" Alice's face was lit with a light I never thought possible in anyone, much less Alice. She looked about the room as though at others gathered there with us. "The pink?" I asked, "You mean the pink we've been working with in our imagery?" "Well, yes, can't you see it? It's everywhere. And see Joan over there—on your left? I want you to meet her." She'd told me in earlier sessions that Joan was a dear friend of hers, one also plagued with lifelong depression, who had died many years ago, still miserable. Joan was now visiting her and telling her that there was nothing to fear. Others were there too, people who had passed on who once were close to Alice—giving her a glimpse of what awaited her in death.

No, I couldn't see the pink, which she said was tinged with a little orange, but I affirmed her view of it and the truth of her experience. Actually, she was the one who convinced me of the truth of it because there's no way I would have believed it if I hadn't seen her glowing eyes. I had heard stories of end-of-life awakenings like this, but wasn't sure I believed in them, and certainly wouldn't have expected it with Alice.

She asked if I would pray with her, something we had never done before. As she began, "The Lord is my shepherd, I shall not want . . ." her voice lightened and began to sing the familiar psalm. She asked me to join her and somehow a voice came through me that wasn't off key and together we sounded like angels, to us at least— and possibly Joan.

She ended by asking me to remember something. "All things are possible," she said. "Yes," I nodded, in my professional, soft, social work voice, which she detected immediately as a front for my disbelief. She narrowed her eyes, looked directly into mine and said, "Look, I mean it. I know it. All things are possible, Diane!" I've never forgotten it either, and many times since then, that statement has helped center me in times of doubt and fear.

I thought that Alice would die soon after that morning, and half expected a call later that day. No, she had a lot more suffering to do in the next month or so. Old doubts, fears and anxieties continued their grip on her, and I continued to listen. Light broke through on occasion as she cleared issues in relationships to her husband and sister, but mostly Alice continued to suffer.

I got the call late one afternoon from the nursing home that death was near for Alice and she was asking for me. Spring had fully arrived outside, but it wasn't apparent in Alice's room that night. The war between the part of her that clung to suffering and the one who trusted the peace of death waged well into the evening and night. Her husband went home exhausted, leaving me alone to sit beside

Alice on her final journey. I, too, was exhausted, but I'd promised her I would stay with her. How could I abandon a woman at death, who had known so much abandonment in life? My *need-to-help* receptors were going wild! I tried everything I knew to ease her passage to death, but nothing helped. She weakly moaned and begged me to relieve her of this pain, over and over and over. Nurses came to check on her vitals, while mine were giving way.

I left her room to seek solitude in the lounge. As I went within, to what I now understand as my Center, a little voice said, "Leave her, go home and sleep." I thought it was just my fatigue talking—my longing to be relieved of this feeling of powerlessness in the face of her suffering. All my studies in both the dying process and energy work failed to guide me through. I'd quiet my mind again, center on my breath, and again the voice would say, "Leave her, go home and sleep."

I knelt at Alice's bedside, took her cool, weak hand in mine and said, "I'm so sorry, Alice, but I have to go home to sleep. I don't know what else I can do to help you. I love you and pray you find peace." I drove home nearly hysterical with tears of failure. I literally fell to my knees in helplessness and grief when I got home.

I awakened as though dead myself and dragged myself into the light of my living room and collapsed on my green leather chair. I knew I had to teach that day (a course on Loss and Grief, no less), and drive the 40 miles to the university, so I began to do an energy exercise that I thought could bring me around. I feebly brought my awareness to each of my chakras (other centers—energetic ones). There are at least seven chakras aligned up the center of our bodies, and this exercise drew my awareness from the lower to the upper ones. Initially, I could hardly find a chakra, much less give it any attention. But as I reached my heart chakra and began to move up from there, I saw Alice, with my inner eye, reaching her arm out to me. I reached toward her, made contact, and then she was gone. My heart seemed to literally swell and expand far beyond my physical body. I continued to move up to the chakra at the top of my head when the phone rang. The nurse said Alice had just died.

On my way to the university, I stopped in Alice's room where her body lay dead. The peace she described weeks earlier was all around her and enfolded me as well. Later, driving east after class as the sun was setting, the clouds spread across the vast horizon of the Kansas prairie to reflect the very shade of pink, just tinged with a little orange that Alice described weeks ago. I knew in my heart that both Alice and I were heading home.

It's not uncommon for your Center to talk to you in times of crisis—when you let go of needing to know or when you've run out of things to do—or simply guide you in a direction that awakens to something new. If I had ignored the inner voice that sent me to her room that Saturday, I would have missed the opportunity to witness Alice's taste of transformation and she wouldn't have had me to share it with, to sing with her. The inner guide that sent me home to rest affirmed my need to center physically, emotionally and spiritually so that I could truly be with Alice as she died.

From those early years working in the rehab hospital to now, I've become increasingly aware of the movement of attention from what's happening "out there" to what's happening within my own biopsychospiritual container and back again. The more flexible I become in the movement between my Center and edge, the healthier my professional relationships become. No boundary between my inner and outer world, but different parts of a whole in relationship. By taking the time to connect to Center, my response to clients helps them find their Center. Once in Center, we are more likely to experience the sixth and last principle of the cell membrane model—Oneness.

Chapter 8

ONENESS

"Nature may be compared to a vast ocean. Thousands and millions of changes are taking place in it. Crocodiles and fish are essentially of the same sub-stance as the water in which they live. Man is crowded together with the myriad other things in the Great Changingness, and his nature is one with that of all other natural things. Knowing that I am of the same nature as all other natural things, I know that there is really no separate self, no separate personality, no absolute death and no absolute life."

- T'ien T'ung-Hsu, 8th Century AD

Nature takes us straight into the paradox of being both separate and one, and invites us to live in full awareness of what the Buddhists call "interbeing," what the Native Americans mean when all ritual is dedicated "to all my relations." Alexander Pope asks us, to "imagine all things and creatures as the cells of a single living being. All are but parts of one stupendous whole, whose body Nature is and God the soul." Arthur Koestler helps us visualize this with his description of living systems as a holarchy. Each part of the whole, whether it's an individual cell or a plant, is a whole system in itself, or holon, which is imbedded within another holon, like the nesting matryoshka dolls from Russia. Each holon, a cell for example, takes care of its own needs while still being in interdependent relationship

Figure 5. Oneness: Interconnected relationships with all life

with the holons within and outside itself. When it comes to healing, you are drawn again and again into the reality of this holarchy.

There's no place to hide in a holarchy, no place you can go without being affected by whatever is happening around you. Likewise, everything we do in our healing relationships is influenced by what's happening around us, and everything around us is influenced by what happens in our healing relationships. I experienced this truth in a profound way one autumn afternoon. Marc, a young practitioner at the retreat center where we both worked, was leaving to return to his native England. I asked him for a session as a way of saying both "thank you" and "farewell." Marc does Waterdance, an aquatic therapy in which you're held in warm water while your body is moved, stretched and massaged both above and below the surface of the water. "No aches or pains," I said, "I just want to experience your great work one more time. I actually feel quite good."

I surrendered to the warm water and the support of his strong body. "Ahh, such peace," I sighed. I always enjoyed the powerful ways that Marc would snake and swoosh my body underwater, making me feel like a piece of kelp bouncing with the ocean's waves, or a sea fan flowing with the current. It was always invigorating to feel the water rush over my skin, tickling all my nerve endings and helping me lose my sense of myself as a land animal. On that late September day in 2001, however, one of those swooshes brought a sensation of being blown from a building and hurled through space by the force of an explosion. I gasped for breath, cried out in terror and shock. Of course I knew I wasn't really falling from a burning building; I was in a warm springs pool in California. Yet, the experience of it felt very real in my body, although in a very nonpersonal way. As Marc gently held and moved me through the water, the terror dissipated entirely, followed by a deep sense of compassion for those whose bodies had been sent flying out of the World Trade Center a couple of weeks earlier. Later in the session, as he gently brought me to the surface of the water, I felt I was being rescued from the rubble, held by someone who cared. My tears of gratitude flowed into the water, which, as I think of it now, eventually found its way to the ocean. I like to think that maybe, just maybe, the energy of my gratitude and compassion is carried by rain that falls on those who drop bombs, in the Great Changingness that T'ien T'ung-Hsu refers to.

In the weeks following 9/11, many came to our retreat center to "get away from the craziness out there." They thought that here, away from television images of loss and destruction, news reports of terrorism and war, they would find refuge from the collective anxiety gripping our world. Many were surprised (as I was in my session with Marc), when feelings of terror, rage and grief came forward as their bodies relaxed in the warm water or on a massage table. Many reported that they had never experienced such intense emotional release before, and the magnitude of it seemed to go way beyond any personal experience they could remember. We cannot separate ourselves from those who either died in the World Trade Center or those who flew their planes into it. I was reminded that when I touch one in healing, I touch all.

46

Science is now catching up to what sages throughout time have revealed about Oneness. When I first read the research of James Oschman, it confirmed why I bristled when therapists talked about the boundaries we set with our clients. His words rang the same bell of truth as the Taoist sages when he wrote, "The boundaries between the cell environment, the cell interior and the genetic material are not as sharp or as impermeable as we once thought." Oschman goes on to describe the cell membrane as a living matrix of fibers and microfilaments that conduct bioelectric energy not only in and out of the cell, but also into the nucleus and genetic material itself. He applies this to healing relationships when he says, "In essence, when you touch a human body, you are touching a continuously interconnected system, composed of virtually all of the molecules in the body linked together in an intricate webwork." As a health practitioner it both humbles and excites me to learn from Oschman that our intentions "give rise to specific patterns of electrical and magnetic activity in the nervous system of the therapist that can spread through their body and into the body of a patient." This web not only responds to our intention, but also carries changes in the Earth's electromagnetic field, influences from solar flares, and other celestial forces.

Buddhist teacher Pema Chödrön reminds us that, "Compassion is not a relationship between the healer and the wounded. It's a relationship between equals." There's no power imbalance as we begin to experience ourselves as individual holons of a single living being. How different would your therapies look and what kind of outcomes would you achieve if you embodied the awareness that the energy of your words and actions can be carried not only throughout your client's bodies, but also through the entire living matrix of which you're a part. If you exploit your clients for personal gain, you exploit yourself. As you bring compassion to the wounds of others, you heal yourself as well.

Oneness fosters interdependent and co-creative healing relationships, while containment and selective permeability prevent the emotional enmeshment that boundaries were created for. All these principles of the cell membrane work together to foster relationships that heal.

A Model for Relationships that Heal

The wisdom of the cell membrane revealed itself to me slowly, over most of my life and continues to tweak my consciousness in my current practice. In this model I've found an effective and reliable guide for managing the complexities and mysteries inherent in healing relationships. Since the principles of the cell membrane are at work in the cells of your body anyway, I hope this journey together will help you awaken to how they're working in your practice. If you look at those best and worst times in your relationships with others through the lens of the cell membrane principles, this model can help you understand why a relationship worked or didn't. It offers you an opportunity to align your practices with the way nature manages all relationships, regardless of culture, language, race or gender.

In summary, the cell membrane principles can help you:

- Recognize and honor the personal and emotional space of your healing partners as you align yourself with all living systems as distinct yet interconnected life forms in a living web.

- Make conscious choices about what you offer and receive from your clients through interspace, creating a relationship field that allows you to interact in clear, yet ever-changing and adaptive ways.

- Respond to a differentiating force that empowers your learning and development as you work within your scope of practice.

- Find your Center when faced with a challenging situation with a client. Each situation demands its own resolution, often in ways that help both you and your clients come to different ways of trusting and understanding.

- Foster integrity in the healing relationship in the awareness that we're all One.

Earlier, I referred to the process by which you differentiated from a single cell in order to embody the complex and highly conscious being that you are. It took all of these principles of containment, selective permeability, interspace, differentiation, centering and one-ness working together to prepare you to bring all your skills, your heart, and yes, your entire history of receptor development, into the healing relationships you form. Because I know that it will take more than reading about this model to embody these principles in your work, I've looked further into how they actually work in my current practice.

In the next section of the book we apply the cell membrane principles from model to healing practice. I offer a five-step process that you can use when questions arise in a session or you get stuck, and then look at how that process can be used to guide us through the many issues we face in practice. We'll now get into where the rubber meets the road in your treatment space.

The Cell Membrane Model
for Healing Relationships

Containment
We support, protect and honor the body, emotions, thoughts
and spirit of our healing partners and ourselves.

Selective Permeability
We make conscious choices about what thoughts, feelings and
intentions move in and out of our personal space, to achieve
flexibility in our response to healing partners.

Interspace
We care for and attend to the safety and co-creative potential
of interspace, the energy field in which a relationship exists.
Both healing partners influence interspace—and are
influenced by it—with their thoughts, feelings and intentions.

Differentiation
We work within our level of training and according to our
professional contract. At the same time, we allow our practice
to grow and evolve new ways of helping.

Connection to Center
We respond to our healing partners from a Centered
position—in our body, emotions, mind and spirit.

Oneness
We relate to our healing partners in the awareness that we are
part of an interconnected web of all life. When we touch one,
we touch ourselves and all other living things.

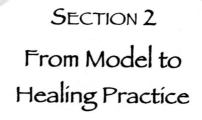

SECTION 2

From Model to
Healing Practice

Chapter 9

FIVE-STEP PROCESS FOR EFFECTIVE PRACTICE

All of life unfolds through relationships that foster (or retard) growth and evolution. If the cell membrane model is to have any value to you, it must meet you where you are in your practice and guide your next evolutionary step. The cell membrane principles revealed themselves over time through relationships with healing partners. It seemed like someone always showed up, especially through the writing of this book, to test my understanding of the principles, to make sure I viewed my practice through the cell membrane's discerning lens. As I tried to teach these principles, or write about them, I looked for how they manifested themselves in my practice. How did I actually live this model in my work? How did my mistakes reveal a departure from the model? I observed that I usually followed five basic steps—steps that took me into containment and selectivity or helped me grow in awareness of interspace or oneness.

Because of the limitations of the written page, I have to list these steps one after the other, but I find, like the cell membrane principles themselves, that each practice situation may call for more attention to one than the other, and that in the end they all work together. You may follow them in a different order than this, but the important thing is to recognize the cell membrane principles at work in each of these steps and to apply them as they fit.

The five-step process I describe here pertains to the *relationship aspects* of healing practices and should be compatible with most modalities. However, if the modality you practice requires an approach that may not fit easily with this process, perhaps one that requires more force or directive influence, I trust that you will adapt it to your circumstances. As you look at the process I use, you may discover that, in your best moments you're already doing something similar to what I'm suggesting in your healing relationships. Your particular training, especially if it's holistic, has probably included some of this. If so, take it as evidence that healing relationships that work, are natural; your practice is aligned with how nature manages relationships. When you're stuck, may the following be a reminder of how you can get into nature's flow again.

A FIVE-STEP PROCESS FOR EFFECTIVE PRACTICE

1. ***What's Happening in Your Healing Partner?***
   Track—Contain—Support
2. ***What's Happening in You?***
   Track—Contain—Support
3. ***Connect to Center***
4. ***What's the Contract?***
   Clarify—Change?
5. ***Respond from Center***

At first glance, this process may look like it would take a long time, but the more you practice, both in and out of sessions, you'll discover that it can often be completed in minutes and repeated several times during a session. Over time it can become fairly automatic, just like the cells of your body. Let's look at each step separately.

Step 1: What's Happening in your Healing Partner?

When you observe what's happening in your partner, you get an idea about what receptors are active in him or her in that moment. We're dealing with basic containment and selective permeability principles here. A change in breath rhythm, a particular comment, movement, or emotion can be a signal that your partner is reacting to something that's happening in the session. His receptors have been activated and his behavior suggests that he's sending a message into inter-space. This reaction may even trigger some kind of a reaction in you, such as concern, anxiety, or a question about how best to respond. Whether you're engaged in bodywork, psychotherapy, or ministry, something is happening in your partner that asks for a response from you. Regardless, of what your partner is doing or saying, it's impor-tant to begin by just observing his experience without judgment. Just note what's there. By doing so, you are following the containment and selective permeability principles, in that you are recognizing what's happening in your partner's personal space and selecting not to take it into your own, even if you notice a reaction in you. (We'll get into your part in a bit.) You are also not sending your judgment into his personal space. Let's tease this containment process out a lit-tle more to see how it works here.

Ron Kurtz, the creator of The Hakomi Method of body-cen-tered psychotherapy, calls this kind of observation, "tracking." Tracking, according to Kurtz, ". . . is looking for signs of the other's present experience." He refers to signs like a sudden rise in the shoulders of a partner, or a funny twitch in the eye. The word "track-ing" pretty well describes what we do in this part of the process—explore what's there to give us signs of what's at work. The phrase "present experience" is essential in this step. We're not interpreting or analyzing what is happening in our partner, wondering if it's a memory or a story. We're just noticing what is there right now: a tear or grimace, a change in posture, etc. Tracking is an open and sensi-tive process, often done with the practitioner bringing awareness and compassion to the process. Whatever your field of practice, this kind of compassionate attention to what is happening with your partner, while you're doing whatever it is you do, can enhance the quality of the relationship. Even if your practice involves analysis or consultation, this compassionate observation sets the stage for what you do next.

By tracking without judgment or interpretation, you bring a level of consciousness into the relationship that helps your partner contain the experience. It's like your attention reinforces his personal membrane. You draw his attention to which receptors are active there—not necessarily by using the term, "receptors," but by saying something like, "I notice you laugh while telling me about something that hurt you," or "What do you notice in your shoulder right now?" In bodywork, you could reflect what you're observing just by adding a little pressure to meet the tension in your partner's joint or muscle. Sometimes, just a genuine sigh or "mmm" let's your partner know you're noticing what's happening.

Remember, *containment invites your partners to be aware of what's happening in them*; you don't receive their experience as yours to do something about. Helping partners to contain their responses brings a level of awareness to their behavior or experience that may never have been there before. Often clients are unaware of what they are showing or even saying, and by simply reflecting it back to them, they become more conscious of what's there. That attention alone is often all that is needed to bring about a shift or release in discomfort for both of you. Of course, you make choices about what's significant and not in what you observe and what you choose to reflect or help contain. I'm not suggesting you mirror everything back so that your partners feel as though they are under a magnifying glass and getting hotter all the time!

Your non-judgmental awareness of what's happening in your client can provide a quality of energy to interspace that supports the safety of the relationship field. In such an environment, your partner is more likely to grow in his awareness of his own experience. Recently, a healing partner was ranting and raving about a marital conflict. I just imagined his words falling into a basket between us, an image of interspace that I find helpful. I didn't want to take all that rage into my personal space, and he certainly wasn't ready to have it sent back to him with a statement, like "I notice you're feeling some rage." I just guided the energy of his rage to settle into the basket, where I could hold it in my compassionate awareness. It wasn't long before he noticed how worked up he was and said, "Wow, I guess I'm still upset, huh?" Then we could attend to his present experience rather than try to fix something that happened last week. Also, by not taking my partner's rage as something I had to do something about, I helped him feel his emotional process in safety, without having it pounced upon right away.

It's important that any attempt you make to track and help contain what's happening in your partner be genuinely connected to your present experience of what you are observing, connected to your heart. While having a script, like " I'm wondering what's . . ." or "I notice that . . ." may help you learn about ways to respond, if you're actually feeling "I don't like the way you . . ." the energy of your dislike moves right through interspace to be picked up by your partner's receptors. It's a delicate process, to be sure, because in the effort to be genuine you don't want to put "I don't like you" into interspace to threaten your partner's security. You can contain and select, however, by saying, "I notice you're . . . , and I'm uncomfortable with that." When you reflect what you're observing and state what's real for you, interspace contains accurate, non-judgmental messages; you've named what's happening in each of your receptors. For example, I recall a time late in a session when my healing partner's body language showed fear, yet she asked if *I* was okay? I knew how fearful she was that she would "wear me out" out like she reported doing with other therapists. Even though I was tired and in need of some centering space, I said, "I'm okay." She looked even more fearful as she searched my eyes for signs of abandonment. In reaction to the fear in her eyes, I made the mistake of insisting I was okay. But I wasn't. Interspace carried my confusing messages (being both okay and exhausted), which continued to trigger her fear. If, instead, I had acknowledged that yes, I was tired and inquired what she was feeling, I could have more directly addressed her fear that I was trying to back out of the healing relationship. Our voice carries the energy of the real feeling, regardless of what's said, right on through the membrane.

You may be asking how do you track and contain something your partner does that you find offensive—something you just don't want to be exposed to. Maybe he's using language you object to or becoming sexually suggestive? Sometimes, his behavior can be subtle, like a casual remark that attributes certain motives or behaviors to you that don't fit. It may even seem like you're being baited, your partner is saying something just to see if you'll bite and take in the message. Statements like, "I notice you are . . ." or "you seem to be saying . . ." help contain the behavior within your partner and indicate that you're not available to receive the message they're sending. Selective permeability allows us to make choices about what we'll receive from a healing partner—or ship the message or projection back to sender. You are not judging your partner's behavior, just reflecting back what you're observing or feeling. Provocative actions from the client sometimes call for following the "What's Happening in You?" and "Connect to Center" processes (described below) before attempting to reflect back to your partner. It's okay to take the time to first take care of yourself, which honors the containment and selective permeability principles as well. We'll get into ways to do this a little later.

Once you track your partner's experience and help her contain it, you can respond in a way to support her present moment experience by being present with it. By support, I mean doing whatever seems indicated to let your partner know that you are available to witness, assist or guide her through the experience. You're not going to take the experience on as your own, but the way you touch, your tone of voice and most of all your compassion and awareness will show your partner that you're right there beside her wherever her experience takes her. If you do psychotherapy or social work, you know that supporting a partner where they are is the first step to taking them to something new, regardless of the theory that guides your practice. In therapies involving touch, you could assist physical or energetic movement that arises, supporting what's ready to happen. Or when you note a change in breath rhythm, you could just follow the breath with awareness or possibly entrain your breath with theirs. In Hakomi and other body-centered practices, the therapist who notices their partner's shoulders rising to the ears might say, "Would it be okay if I held your shoulders for you for a little bit?" I've been amazed at the shifts that happen with these simple gestures of support.

It's beyond the scope of this book to suggest specific supportive practices that relate to a specific modality, but I do want to emphasize the value of support for the present moment experience of your partner—even if what you are facing feels like resistance. If your partner is resisting treatment in any way, you gain nothing by pushing against the resistance or running away from it, as you've likely discovered. In the chapter on Power and Control in the Healing Relationship, I spend more time on working with resistance, but the basic principle is to support it in your partner until it feels safe to move through resistance to something else.

Should an intense emotional release occur in a session, you can let your partner know you are aware of what they're feeling through the quality of your voice or touch. It's important that you just meet her release at the intensity in which she is experiencing it and not try to intensify or reduce it. You don't want to charge up sadness by dramatically saying, "Boy, that's really terrible, isn't it?" Each of us reacts to particular emotions in our own way, and we don't want to impose our emotional process onto our partners. We just need to check out where the energy of this person's emotion (emotion = energy in motion) wants to go and help it get there. Ron Kurtz calls this kind of support, "riding the rapids" with someone. Just follow along, without adding force to either propel or stop what is happening. If you've checked out your own reaction and act from Center (see below), you're more likely to respond in a way that supports what's ready to happen with your partner.

To summarize, once you've observed something happening in your partner that seems to be significant to their healing process or is uncomfortable for either of you, you can:

- Track you partner's experience
- Help her/him contain it
- Support you partner's process

By simply checking out and supporting what's happening in your partner, you are aligning your practice with primarily the containment and selective permeability principles of the cell membrane. In addition, by paying attention to what's happening in interspace, the energetic highway between you, and holding what's there in compassion and non-judgment, the Oneness principle comes in to play. Differentiation can happen, as well, as your partner's receptors respond to non-reaction and compassion. These same principles apply when it's *your* inner reaction that's asking for support. Let's look at what's possible when you answer the question: What's Happening in You?

Step 2: What's Happening in You?

Observe what thoughts, feelings or sensations arise in you in response to what you perceive in your partner. Sometimes your process needs attending to before you can support him. Again, it's important to observe your feeling without judgment. Just because you're there to help another doesn't mean whatever you're feeling merits any less consideration than what your partner is up to. Besides, it's impossible to develop a non-judgmental or non-reactive approach unless you begin by practicing non-judgment on yourself. By simply noticing what's there, you are tracking your own experience and working with the containment and selective permeability principles, but you can also track where in your body that you're feeling the reaction. What exactly are those receptors saying to you? "Hey, you jerk! Now you've gotten yourself into a fix!" or "This feels just like Mom, and I don't like it!" or "This feels pretty slimy!" Can you listen to them with the same compassion you expect of yourself with others? If so, you're more likely to contain the response without shooting off reactive messages into the space between you. As long as you're paying attention to your own feeling, it can't act like a loose cannon in interspace setting off your partner's receptors.

I've inadvertently tested this kind of personal containment over and over—and maybe you have too. Sometimes when I'm bored, my mind wanders to what it is I have to do when I get home, is there anything in the fridge to eat—that kind of stuff. My body and hands keep working somehow, but my mind is focused on something else. As often happens in these sessions, the person says, "That was the best session I ever had! Your hands went just where I needed." Obviously, my thoughts, contained by my attention to them, weren't floating in interspace. I found that when I was doing just talk therapy, one part of me was listening, tracking what was happening in my partner, while another part, a part I call a "witness," noticed how I was reacting to what I heard and contained it. I remember one time an elderly woman was accusing me of something I knew I hadn't done. While I listened to her accusations calmly, another part of me witnessed thoughts like, "Damn, what do I do now?" and "How the heck did she get that idea?" Of course, if I verbalized those fears, it wouldn't have served her or me, so I contained and supported my own process first before I could help her contain hers. Soon, with only her emotions held in interspace, she came to realize something she'd long forgotten—as a child, she'd been hurt in ways she was now accusing me of. I didn't have to defend myself or try to appease her, just help her feel more of what was happening in her and it took her to a new understanding.

Sometimes we get reactive just at the sight of our partner, without him having to do anything at all. He may look threatening or in one particular bodywork situation I remember—darned attractive! My *hot guy* receptors were jumpin' all over the place. "Oh, no, not allowed," I told myself, and pushed them out of my mind. He responded to my touch with sighs of satisfaction and even a slight erection. Whew, finally the session was over and he was on his way. The next week he was back! As he smiled seductively and slowly lowered his handsome body to the massage table, I got the idea (cell membrane talkin' to me) that maybe I should just let myself observe those beautifully sculpted muscles, feel my attraction and watch it. In less than ten minutes he was snoring! No sighs of pleasure; he left feeling relaxed and not visibly aroused. More importantly, after just a few minutes of watching and containing my desire, it just dissipated. It was no big deal, just a momentary attraction that in the previous week grew in intensity when I tried to slap a boundary around it. Of course, there may have been other factors influencing those two sessions, but for me, the way I responded to my desires was the key to skillful response and self-awareness.

In that second session with this attractive man, I tracked my desire, supported it with my non-judgmental awareness and it didn't get in the way of the healing relationship. Note also that because I was aware of the feeling and kept it in my awareness (containment), there was an element of choice (selective permeability) that isn't available when you don't know what's active—or try to suppress it. Suppressed emotions seem to find their way into interspace, but awareness contains them. When we can support and not judge our emotions, we're no longer at their mercy. Let's look at some of the options you have for supporting yourself when faced with fears, desires and longings.

Breathe consciously

You might explore the power of your own breath as a source of support. When you're anxious or scared you may stop breathing, holding in and holding back. Breath brings vital energy into what's ready to be known, while also helping to calm the anxiety. Years ago, I called my friend, a minister, for help as I prepared to get on a plane to be at my father's bedside as he was dying. Dave's only advice to me was to remember to breathe. As I looked into the frightened, jaundiced eyes of my father, that advice not only got me through the week of his dying, but it provided the fear and grief with a pathway out, to be replaced by the vital energy I so needed. When you breathe into a feeling, it can also take you more deeply into what's underneath the feeling. When your mind is on your breath, the feelings are not acting on your partner. You're not taking action on the feeling, just being with it, trusting it and inquiring of it. You do this from the perspective of a compassionate observer in the spirit of inquiry, not judgment. The intention is to bring what may be unconscious into your awareness. It's a way of knowing what receptors have been triggered by the interaction. Whether you touch or talk in your work, taking the time to breathe consciously can often be all you need to dissipate the anxiety, and it doesn't have to take very long.

Color

In and out of sessions, you might want to ask if there's a specific color that could be brought to the place of anxiety. Most people are surprised to find that even if they've never worked with color for healing or know anything about it, just through this simple act of asking for a color, they get a sense of just the right color coming to them. Colors carry specific vibrations that can be just what you need. You don't have to actually see the color. If I asked you what "green" felt like, I'm sure you could get some sense of it. You would know how different green is from red, for example, by knowing what each color feels like to you. It's not even helpful to think about the quality of a particular color, because we, and a whole bunch of experts have lots of ideas about that. Each color has its own vibrational signature, so it's about trusting that your receptors know just the vibration they need to be able to shift to a less anxious state.

Link with support

Another kind of self-support that you can turn to when you need it in challenging situations comes along the energetic highway, from the interspace that you share with a supportive friend, your higher self, a teacher, a spiritual guide, mentor, or a parent. Interspace exists beyond time and space, as we're told by quantum physicists and consciousness researchers, so the energy of compassion, wisdom and acceptance that you feel with this other being can be present with you while you struggle in another relationship. I sometimes work in a team of people I really trust to support me and to offer their healing gifts when I need them. In difficult sessions, where I'm stuck and don't know what to do, I often feel like one or more of these folks is standing right there beside or across from me. They help me find that place in me that knows what to do or say.

It may seem like this step of tracking, containing and supporting your own process would take a long time and be hard to do while still mobilizing a shoulder joint, or in the face of an emotional episode with your partner. The more you practice this 5-step process in and out of sessions, especially the easy ones, the easier and quicker it becomes in the heat of the moment. In between sessions, you can do this as a kind of imagery exercise in which you bring your awareness back to a situation, and imagine it's happening now. Then you can take the time you need to practice the steps and arrive at a centered response. When I do this, I'm often surprised at where the inner inquiry takes me, and it's usually quite helpful. When I practice these steps during a session, it's always amazing to me how my partner's process does seem to stay in its own track as I take care of myself. You may be wondering, with all this attention to what's happening in you, "Isn't this supposed to be about the client, after all?" Yes, of course it is, but according the cell membrane principles, both partners are active in bringing awareness to what is presented for healing in the relationship. When you practice self-awareness in sessions, inner calm can often be restored very quickly, which naturally takes you to the next step: Connect to Center.

Step 3: Connect to Center

Tension and anxiety often yield to the containment, tracking and support steps we've just looked at. Attending to the tempest often takes you to the calm center where thoughts and feelings are no longer swirling around you. You may already be quite practiced at finding that place within to guide your work with others. You may have discovered that, over time, centering becomes the foundation of all you do. Yet finding your center can be challenging at times.

One of the dimensions of center is the physical one. How am I standing in my own body? I center myself by bringing my awareness to the alignment of my spine, the position of my neck and shoulders and which direction my feet and knees are facing. From here, I feel better prepared to meet whatever movement (physical or emotional) I'm encountering with my partner. I know from my experience as a receiver of bodywork, that if the giver is grounded and centered in her body, the receiver feels it and it helps him come to center as well. Even if you're just standing at a patient's bedside or sitting across a room, by softening your body and centering in your physical being you can calm a situation and allow for a more healing exchange. Physical centering contributes to the quality of the healing relationship container and invites your partner into safer space.

A body of knowledge, a therapeutic contract (see more on this below), standards of practice, and codes of ethics, also provide us with the guidance we need when we're off-center. Taking time to bring your attention to what it is you're doing in the moment, what's the contract, and what do the body of professionals you associate with expect of you can be great centering tools. When you're floating in uncertainty, you can intentionally anchor your mind on what you know in the moment and then act from there. But sometimes, your thinking self may seem to be hostage to the emotional juices rising inside.

Emotional centering can be a little more difficult, but it helps if you start out solidly present in your own body. Emotional energy can take your awareness literally out of your body where it can get very tangled up with what's happening in your client. Once you consciously move your awareness into your body, bringing breath to where the emotion is registering in your body, you can more easily connect to center.

As I noted earlier, suppression doesn't work very well when you're trying to respond skillfully to challenging situations, even though many of us were told to "leave our feelings at the door" before entering our treatment space. It takes energy to keep whatever we're feeling out of our awareness, and that energy shows up as tension in interspace. A friend recently told me about his relationship with a therapist who just experienced the death of her sister. He knew about it because she had to cancel an appointment the previous week. In their next appointment, he asked his therapist how she was doing. She just tightened up and said, "Let's keep our focus on what's happening with you." All he felt was tension in the space, he said, and therefore did not feel safe to be real with her in what he was feeling. He didn't want her to fill the space with her own grief, necessarily, but he hoped she would at least acknowledge it was there and not hold on so tight. Her vulnerability was not disturbing to him, but her tension was. What if, instead, she had told him she was having a rough time since her sister's death, took a deep breath, just sat silent for a while and then refocused on his problem? I think they would each have been drawn to center. Breathing into a feeling, rather than suppressing it, often offers a portal to deeper levels of awareness that can lead you to Center. From there you can discover the most healing response just bubbling up.

Your Center may be your awareness of God, Goddess, a higher power or even your mission in life. Something bigger than the emotional quandary you currently find yourself in can help you find the Center within. In Chapter 7, I talked about my work with Alice, the woman who wanted me to help her die. When I finally listened to the little voice in my Center which told me to go home and rest, I was led to discover there were other ways of being with her when she died, while also enhancing my trust in a process bigger than what I could control. It also helped me find and trust Center the next time I was in a fix.

This "Connecting to Center" may seem pretty complex or even demanding when all you're trying to do is get out of a tough situation. After all, how can you think about your body, your training, your breathing or even God when what you really want is a way out? The road to Center actually takes you through rather than out of a problem. Centering requires practice and as you grow in your ability to travel there and experience the bumps in the road, each trip gets easier. Center might start showing up spontaneously as an intuitive hunch, or just as a gentle mist that softens the sharp peaks of the emotional waves. With practice you can become quite adept at finding your inner guide, your Center. As you cultivate a relationship between your Center and the receptors that get activated with difficult clients, your ability to connect to Center will improve. You will more readily move between what's happening on the outside with what's happening on the inside.

Practice connecting to Center outside of sessions. The better you get in these practice sessions, the easier it will be to center yourself in sessions with a client. Regular practice with centering exercises, meditation and prayer will help (See the Resources section at the end of the book) You can also work on your centering through Tai Chi, Qi Gong, Yoga or Ai Chi and other movement and awareness practices to help you become both more mindful and centered. Starting a workday with these practices and beginning a session from a centered position will enable you to act more responsibly and less reflexively to difficult situations that could arise in your practice.

Sometimes, however, after a period of intense work with clients, we need to retreat somewhere to find our Center again. For me, I often take a walk alone or drive to the ocean or another place in the wild that nurtures and energizes my Center. Such nurture often takes the form of finally having the time to be with whatever is up for me in my life, or clear the energy that's blocking my access to Center. What's happening in my personal space that's being activated in my sessions? I might do self-healing exercises or journal—or just sit quietly in the wilderness. With my inner resources renewed, I can be where I need to be with clients. To seek therapy, consultation and/or supervision is also an excellent centering practice.

Whatever it is you do to find and nurture your Center, the important thing is to do it—often. You can't help anyone if you're off-center.

Step 4: What's the Contract?

A contract—an agreement between you and the client about what they want from you and what you are willing and able to provide—offers another kind of center in the therapeutic relationship. From the cell membrane model's perspective, the contract serves to identify which of your receptors will be open and available to the relationship and also serves as its container. Whether the treatment setting involves very explicit, written and signed contracts, or more informal agreements, *it's important to center the relationship in a mutual understanding of why you're both there.*

When you're not quite sure how to respond when something unexpected arises in a session or course of treatment, it's helpful to refer to the contract. How does the current situation fall within the agreed upon focus of treatment? Does something have to be clarified or changed? Again, you're asking for clarification on which receptors, from the cell membrane's perspective, are currently active, and making choices about whether you need to redirect attention based on the original contract? If it no longer fits, then you may need to discuss a change. Contracts evolve as relationships and healing outcomes evolve, and the selective permeability and differentiation principles help us respond moment-by-moment to what receptors need to open or close and how a contract may need to change.

Rarely, one or both partners can no longer abide by the contract and the relationship or individual session needs to be terminated. These situations also clarify which receptors you each can or cannot make available to the relationship. For example, if a partner asks for something I'm not prepared for, either through training or willingness, I can simply say, without judgment, that I'm not prepared for what she is asking. Similarly, if my partner isn't prepared for a level of participation I'm asking for, she can suggest a change or termination. The termination could be communicated as a poor fit, rather than someone's failure. Again, the cell membrane model informs us that this is a matter of resonance and selectivity, not either partner's problem alone.

Step 5: Respond from Center

I've already noted how essential it is that your response to a client comes from a centered position after you've brought consciousness to the feelings the session evokes. If you feel immediately threatened, a reflexive response may be justified, that is, you need to take immediate action. But even here, you owe it to yourself and the client to check out how real your perception of the threat actually is. The words and gestures you put into interspace can be powerful. All the other cell membrane principles apply here. I've heard both clients and therapists describe situations in which they were sure the other was threatening or provoking them in some way, only to learn later, after going within and then to Center, that an old receptor was being activated without an actual threat. It's always helpful to check out the projection process and where it's taking the relationship.

Connecting to and acting from Center takes you out of your habitual reactivity to tweaked receptors and moves you into action that comes from a higher dimension of your being. Let me explain further. If my client triggers some anger in me, for example, one of my anger receptors is buzzing in alarm wanting quick relief. If it's my habit to react to anger by either withdrawing or attacking, then that's what I'll do, if I don't take care of my anger in another, more effective way. Once in Center, I'm better able to bring a higher level of response to the person who triggered the anger. Both of us benefit. Centering allows you to move beyond your personal anxiety to meet your client with greater compassion, which usually results in a more skillful healing practice.

~~~~~~

I once had an initial session with a man who really irritated me with everything he was doing and saying. It was an aquatic bodywork session, so I had time to go more consciously through this process because I didn't have to be talking to him all the time. I'd notice what he was saying or gesturing or how his body was moving and I really got triggered. Boy, did his behavior surface some nasty feelings in me! I watched each receptor as it voiced its ire, and each one took me deeper into feelings of surprisingly intense anger and disgust, which I watched, breathed into and stumbled my way through on my way to Center. "Ah, Center, this feels good," I thought, just before another lob came my way. Oh, how I wanted to fire back a slam! Or dunk him! But, no, I was trying to put this cell membrane model into practice, so I watched, breathed and Centered again . . . and again . . . and again. Finally, nothing he sent my way could knock me off center. When I felt firmly in Center, I lifted his head, so he could hear me, and calmly asked him to just notice the messages he was sending my way as though he were speaking and gesturing to himself. We completed the session in silence. As he thanked me for the work, there was no hint in him or me of either the messages he was sending or the anger it provoked in me.

It would have been entirely in line with the cell membrane principles to terminate this same session, to state what I was and was not comfortable with. But I wanted to grow in my ability to respond from Center and facilitate co-creative healing. He gave me the chance to practice. If I terminated the session before centering fully, anything I said would have carried judgment and anger right through interspace and into his cells. Instead, I got to notice how much wrath I'm capable of and he got a better idea of what he was doing—which he could choose to pay attention to or not. Selective permeability and differentiation gives us the flexibility to decide to what extent we want to explore the healing potential in any given situation.

That particular session grew out of lots of practice with this process over quite a few years. It also grew out of my intention to understand and put into practice what the cell membrane was teaching me. Each time, over the years, when I took a few minutes to track, contain and support whatever I observed in my partner or myself, connect to and respond from Center, it made it easier to do it the next time. And there are still times when I think it won't work; I'm stuck and that's it. So it's a process I continue to grow into, and you can, too.

Depending on the level of relationship complexity you face in your practice, it may take seconds or several minutes within a session to take yourself through the inner work needed to arrive at a skillful response. It can simply become the way you work, not just in response to difficult situations. You may want to slowly take yourself through these steps alone after the session, or with the help of a colleague or teacher, to help you process what the session awakened. I've found that the principle of resonance attracts partners to my practice that take me to just where I need to be in my inner work to take me to that next level of skill. The key is observation, practice, and acceptance of whatever you discover in yourself and those you help. This five-step process can become automatic. You probably recognize you are doing a good bit of this already.

The cell membrane model and this five-step process help me create a whole new context for the common themes that show up in healing relationships, sometimes as problems or ethical dilemmas. I'll continue this reflective journey by illustrating how the practice of these principles and the five-step process can work for you as you:

- create a safe and sacred space for you and your healing partner
- work with power and control issues
- enhance the resource balancing potential of money
- navigate the pitfalls and potential in dual relationships
- tap into the healing potential of sexuality

Again, like the cell membrane principles themselves, which all interact in relationships, many of these issues arise in and interact with each other in your healing sessions. However, since the pages of a book ask that we deal with them one at a time, we'll start with how the cell membrane model helps to create a safe space.

Chapter
10

CREATING A SAFE AND SACRED SPACE FOR HEALING

As I descended the wooden ladder into a kiva, I felt earth all around me as the sun-warmed adobe walls held me in sacred space. The kiva, the lower chamber of the cliff dwellings in the Mesa Verde ruins was a ceremonial place for the ancient pueblo people, a container for healing. They regularly cleansed the kiva with sage and invoked the spirits of the four cardinal directions in preparation for ceremony. As I sat there, it was as though I'd dropped into the interspace of these ancient healing relationships. Kivas work like cell membranes work. They provide a safe, contained space. Like the openings in the cell membrane, a kiva also has a small opening, called a *sipapu*, through which light and spiritual energy passes to support the sacred rituals contained inside. The kiva formed the container in which the shaman and those coming for healing came together in interspace.

I was reminded of my experience in the kiva when I read Jim Gilkeson's *Energy Healing: A Pathway to Inner Growth*, in which he suggests we can create an energetic kiva in our healing relationships. He wasn't suggesting you dig a deep hole in the earth, but when you attend to all the dimensions of your healing space, the physical, emotional and spiritual, you follow this rich tradition of the pueblo people. Ritual spaces, like kivas, sweat lodges and other indigenous healing spaces seem to embody the cell membrane model principles as follows:

- Containment, in which we create a structure of some kind that supports the healing process, protects those inside from harm, while helping them feel the power of their own experience within their personal container.

- Selective permeability, that tells us we have choices about what each partner contributes to the healing space, what's expected of each of us.

- Interspace, where attention is paid to the thoughts, feelings and intentions that get carried along the energetic highway between healing partners and the space around them.

- Differentiation, which fosters the evolution of new skills and qualities in participants, keeping the healing space alive and flexible.

- Centering in the trust that something bigger than, yet also within each one of the partners and the space they create together will guide the healing process.

- Oneness, that tells us that the safe and sacred space we create for one relationship touches all others, that we dedicate it to "all my relations."

The primary function of the cell membrane is to create an environment in which individual cells can function at their optimum while also maintaining homeostasis within the systems of which they are a part. So, of course, it can tell us a lot about the physical, emotional and spiritual environment in which healing relationships function. Like our professional codes of ethics that serve to protect vulnerable clients from a practitioner's (or health system's) abuse of power, the cell membrane protects the cell's interior. At the same time, the cell membrane does more; it goes beyond the protective, fear-based function to manage a balance of power in the system—it maintains homeostasis. Safe space, from the cell membrane perspective, means a space that is not only free from harm, but one that restores balance and growth in awareness that we are whole and interconnected beings. Let's look more closely at how these principles of the cell membrane function to help you create a safe and sacred space for your healing relationships.

From what we've been considering so far in this exploration of nature's model for healing relationships, let's go on an imaginary journey into what safe and sacred space can look like. Let's assume for this journey that there are two healing partners, you and the one who has come to you for help. Each of you arrives wrapped in separate containers that hold your respective histories and your potential. That wrapping, like a cell membrane, is selectively permeable. Your bodies and the energy fields that encompass them begin to resonate with each other, and interspace is created out of that energetic interaction. You engage each other in some kind of physical environment—an office, clinic, hospital room, chapel or outdoor space— that supports the healing process. Within this physical space some kind of healing modality is performed, a ritual of sorts. All of this— your physical and energetic bodies, the messages flowing through interspace, the work you do together and the physical space that holds it all together—comprise the healing space, just as the cell membrane holds all the activities of the cell together. Safety and sacredness arise from the contribution of all these parts.

We humans have always recognized the healing value of safe and sacred space. Native people, in constructing kivas, understand that a place needs to be set apart, yet connected to the whole, to contain healing rituals that take place apart from ordinary activities of daily living. Care is taken by healers of all varieties to bring into the space only that which supports healing. Starting with intention, let's look at some of the factors that contribute to safe and sacred space and how the cell membrane model can guide its formation.

Intention

Intention sets the stage for what will happen in healing encounters and dedicates the space to that purpose. Both partners, of course, bring an intention, which begins to permeate interspace right from the start. Marilyn Schlitz, a leading consciousness scientist at the Institute of Noetic Sciences, in Petaluma, CA defines intention as "the projection of awareness, with purpose and efficacy, toward some object or outcome." The awareness you project grows out of your own self-development and the skills you've acquired. Intention fills interspace with the emotional and spiritual energy from which the relationship unfolds, and leads to the techniques you choose, how you design the physical space, etc. Intention forms the blueprint for the kiva.

You may want to recall an intention you bring to your healing space, or to a particular healing relationship. Which of your receptors will you call into the service of that intention? What qualities do you decide to project through touch, talk or awareness into the interspace you share with your partner? Which ones will you hold in the background? What tools will you need? For example, you engage those receptors or inner resources that relate to healing function, like compassion and/or knowledge of human anatomy. Intention literally helps you focus your work on what you're there to do, and nothing else, just as clearly as a cell membrane is equipped with receptors of just the right shape and vibration to carry out its specific task. By setting an intention to facilitate healing, the receptors you've chosen go to work with your Center to bring the energy of that intention into the relationship field where they contribute to the quality of the healing space. Your receptors listen and your Center responds with compassion, the right kind of touch or a kind word.

Intention and Outcome

Lynne McTaggert, in her book, *The Intention Experiment*, reviews the extensive research on intention, which supports what I've observed about the effect of intention on healing. McTaggert reports how, in a connected relationship, the one with the clearest, most coherent intention can profoundly influence the outcome. Remember, nature wants to move towards balance, so the one with the intention most aligned with the healing direction of the system, will help the more imbalanced, or chaotic one come into balance. The strength and clarity of your intention, therefore, does more than create (or destroy) a safe space, it can in many cases be the most operative tool you use.

Evolving Intention

McTaggert's research demonstrates that, "attention, belief, motivation, and compassion are important for intention to work." It's important that both partners be as clear as is possible at the outset what they're there for and what they believe about what's happening. I've discovered, however, that more often than not the real intention often isn't revealed until well into the healing process. Or it seems that the setting of one intention invites deeper, more fundamental intentions to surface. Carolyn, a middle-aged mother of three, helped me see how an intention can work to invite intention to evolve. When I started to work with Carolyn many years ago, she had already devoted over 10 years to surviving metastatic breast cancer. By using every tool available to conventional and complementary medicine, she thought she had "beaten it," when she discovered another lump in her breast. I met Carolyn when I gave a talk to her cancer support group, and she hoped that in energy work she'd found something new to beat it again. Her intention was to beat cancer. While I shared her intention to survive, my larger intention was, as it usually is, to facilitate healing wherever and however it progresses.

In the course of our work, I learned that Carolyn was the youngest of nine children, and the only one who hadn't been either physically or sexually abused by their father. She grew up, married, had children and was living a happy life—until she got cancer. The energy work helped Carolyn discover a hidden intention—one that lay under the very successful 10-year focus to stay alive. She was surprised to discover a need to suffer, as her siblings had. As the hidden intention to suffer joined the one directed to beating cancer, she uncovered an even deeper one—the need she had to be connected to her siblings. By not being abused, she didn't feel like one of them; she didn't belong. Over the last 10 years, she had gathered them around her suffering with surgery, chemotherapy, shark cartilage, diet, etc., and felt like she finally belonged. I helped her to understand (with the cell membrane interspace and oneness principles in mind) that the energy of the abuse, and even the unconscious pain of her abusive father flowed in the interspace of her family—they all lived in the same pot of soup. She was never apart from that. In her healing, by moving through the pain of the abuse, she found that the light of love also infused the family soup. Carolyn no longer saw her body's recurring cancer as her failure to beat cancer, and she directed her awareness to a new intention to fully experience the love of her family as long as she lived. She engaged her brothers and sisters in eventually creating a loving space for her dying. During her last weeks, she asked me to visit her at home. I approached the house sadly, thinking I would find people deep in the grief of her last days. Instead, I found peace. Family members were tending to various chores with joy as Carolyn lay in her bed, free of pain. The fight was over and she was surrounded by love, knowing she belonged.

You can see, then, that since intention is directed awareness, the more awareness grows, the larger your intention has to be to hold the space for your partner's evolving intentions. My intention with Carolyn included, but wasn't limited by, her intention to beat cancer; it focused my awareness on her overall healing process. Questions arise as I reflect on this in light of the recent research on intention. What could have happened if both of us narrowed our initial intention toward the cell-by-cell destruction of the tumors, now dispersed all through her body? Research certainly supports the effectiveness of highly specific and clear intentions, and Carolyn had successfully combated tumors for 10 years with that kind of directed intention. Yet during those 10 years, she lived in fear. She did little else but focus on her cancer, and by her own admission was not connected to her husband, children and life in general in a way that was fulfilling. Her intention to survive didn't allow room for living. By holding survival within the overall intention of healing we gave it more space to allow other healing opportunities to surface around it. The point is, that intention takes the lead in creating the energy of interspace so that whatever is ready to come forward for healing, there'll be a receptor on board to catch it.

Evolving intentions seem to be quite consistent with the cell membrane model of nature's way with healing, where cells are always responding to changes in the environment and differentiating to meet new opportunities and challenges. The research that proves the power of directed thoughts and awareness in making profound changes in tissues, must, by the very nature of research, narrow the parameters of observation to get clear and statistically significant results. The intention of the research is to inquire of the phenomenon of intention, so of course those narrow parameters are necessary. However, if our healing intent is to help someone restore balance in a system while they become more aware of their interconnectedness with all life, we have to pay attention to how the intention evolves as the awareness evolves. The quality and size of the space in which we hold healing intentions either limits them or allows them to evolve.

Authentic vs. Synthetic Intention

The various receptors on the cell membrane can sometimes be tricked into receiving a message that prevents the real message from getting through. For example, there are synthetic chemicals that look and "sound" enough like the real thing—a natural hormone, for example. When the synthetic binds with the receptor for that natural hormone, it prevents the real thing from latching on or having its authentic message transmitted. A synthetic transmitter molecule can also distort the message and therefore the response by the cell. Intentions can do the same thing. I took a workshop several years ago in which the leader talked a lot about his intention to create a safe space for the participants, a space in which we could feel safe in getting in touch with "the music within" and give it expression. He skillfully chose his words, sending just the right sounding messages into the group interspace, bathing all our *fear of expression* receptors or those that might be afraid of finding our song. My receptors began to question the authenticity of his words, but the words were so right and good, and felt so much like the assuring words my *fear of singing* receptors wanted to hear. So I squelched the doubts, and told myself that they merely signaled my resistance to this whole thing I have about musical expression.

Then I watched the leader really pushing one of the participants to go deep inside to find his sound. It was not the "invitation" he had talked about earlier, but was clearly insensitive to what the participant was actually experiencing. The space felt anything but safe for the one being pushed or those of us watching. The leader's skillful verbal messages were beginning to dislodge from my receptors, which waited instead for a more authentic transmission. His hidden intention to push us into expression colored interspace with a less than safe hue.

The challenge of intention

So, if the healer's intention is so important to the relationship, doesn't that place an extraordinary burden on the healer to be aware and clear? Well, fortunately the selective permeability and differentiation principles jump in to help. The workshop leader got enough messages through his receptor field that we weren't feeling safe, that he eventually had to differentiate a little from his usual pitch to meet us where we were. He had to slow down, let our responses register in interspace, and approach our delicate fears of expression with a little more compassion and less push. He had to really honor the integrity of our personal space within the safe space he talked about. His stated intention had to become more real.

If you set an intention to support someone through a healing crisis, for example, and you know from the cell membrane model that you have receptors that can be activated by the situation, you'll be better prepared to notice the resonance. You're less likely to be caught by surprise when your partner's needs trigger some of your own. You may discover a hidden intention you didn't know was lurking in the background of your consciousness. That awareness can help you become more clear about your intention. By watching receptors as they squawk, and make decisions about how you want to grow and differentiate with this work, you will be better able to form intentions that are congruent with the needs of the healing partnership.

An example of such an intention challenge occurred not long ago. Another aquatic bodywork teacher referred a man to me for a therapeutic session. She mentioned that he might be interested in training in aquatic energy work, a new course I was teaching. When he was so receptive to the work, my *student recruiter* receptor started saying, "Hey, wouldn't you love this guy in your class?" I noticed a shift in my intention, then—and the focus of the work. I wanted to impress him with the nature of the work as well as meet his healing needs, so the intention became less clear. Once in my awareness, I made the choice to focus instead on the broader intention of his healing in this session and not flood interspace with my desire to attract good students; I contained it. Work with the cell membrane model prepared me for that kind of directed awareness. It also helped me reside in the trust that if his being a student in my class was good for both of us, and the school of which we were a part (oneness principle), he'd find his way into my class. He didn't, and that was fine, but I rested in the knowledge that I was as aware and clear as I could be about my intention in his therapeutic session. It's important that I hear the "as I could be" part, so that I'm not too hard on myself when those hidden intentions come forward. After all, that's what the differentiation process is there for—to help me expand what I could be.

Now that we've looked at the key role of intention in the creation of our kiva, the safe space in which we meet our healing partners, we're ready to go the next step. It may already be obvious to you, but self-awareness plays a key role in the authenticity and clarity of our intentions.

Self-Awareness

Since intention is directed awareness, it's clear that awareness of who you are and what you're there for plays a fundamental role in the creation of safe and sacred space. I often do an exercise in my classes where students ask each other the repeating question, "What motivates you to do this work?" for five to seven minutes. In answer to the question over and over, students move from answers like, "It's a better profession than what I've been doing." Or, "It gives me a chance to help people grow and heal," to those closer to the bone, such as, "I want to touch people," or "I want to nurture." Some are motivated by wanting what they think is a lucrative profession, a way to make money. Still others are seeking spiritual connection. The students squirm a little when I say that your core motivations identify those longings that can, if unknown and uncontained, sneak into the healing space you're trying to create with clients. If your healing partners are the only outlet for your touch or nurture, interspace can be clouded by your needs. If income is your main motivator, what will you compromise to get it? If you piggyback on your client's spiritual process, the clarity of their spiritual experience and therefore healing space is compromised.

Exercises like this help you explore the selective permeability, interspace and differentiation principles of the cell membrane model. The exercise draws your awareness within to see which receptors are activated by the question, some of which you may not have known about. Once you discover a hidden motivation or intention, that awareness can guide your selectivity with regard to what you'll place in interspace, or give you an idea of what messages you may be sending unconsciously into interspace. Maybe you could try this repeating question with a trusted colleague, one with whom you feel safe. You can begin by setting the intention to really discover your core motivation. Once you come to your final answer, explore how that motivation currently shows itself in your healing relationships. What do you need to do to support yourself in that motivation? To take care of yourself and not ask your partners to do it for you? How will just the increased awareness help you differentiate your practice so that your needs get met while fostering healing in your partners? When I first tried this exercise as a participant in a workshop, I finally came to the answer, "because I'd die if I didn't do it." Wow! I didn't know that was there. It sure did help me understand the anxiety I felt when I had no sessions scheduled for the day! Further exploration helped me realize that this wasn't about a fear of not having money to keep me alive, but that the value of my life was at least partially related to the opportunity to give expression to my healing gifts. By simply becoming aware of that, I felt more compassion for myself and less needy of my clients to affirm my value. The need differentiated into an affirmation of a life purpose that continues to be redefined all the time.

Interactions with your healing partners can function much in the way the repeating question can—in fact it sometimes feels that way. When one client after another, for example, triggers the same receptors in you, isn't that kind of like a repeated question, targeting an issue, quite specifically, that wants your attention? For example, just as my elderly mother was slipping more deeply into dementia, one client after another presented some aspect of neediness that took me more deeply into my core experience around my mother's needs and my lifelong responses to them. I wasn't depending on my clients to deal with my personal issues, but I knew through our interactions that my receptors around neediness could unconsciously release messages that flavored the interspace I shared with them. Their needs and my reaction to neediness were in resonance, inviting each of our receptors into a vibrational conversation. As the therapist, my responsibility to hold safe and sacred space asked that I track, contain and support my own process around these issues. The cell membrane model, by guiding me to favor awareness over suppression, invited me to look at my own issues. You probably have a list of your own issues that come up repeatedly. Every time the various issues that arise around money, sex, parenting, etc. come up, they invite us into greater awareness of the opportunity to bring clarity and safety to interspace.

Of course, the client's self-awareness contributes to the safety of the healing space as well. Especially in bodywork practices, where intimate touch is involved, a client may think they're seeking relief from tension, for example, when a not-so-conscious part of them longs for sensuous touch, or even erotic stimulation. A psychotherapy client may not realize he's looking forward to talking to you as much out of loneliness as anything else he may be presenting. Again, the cell membrane principle of containment guides us to foster awareness in our partners by reflecting back to them what we're noticing, rather than either ignoring or setting an artificial boundary around those underlying intentions.

Clarity of Contract

Clear intention and self-awareness naturally lead to clarity in the contract you form with your healing partners. I introduced the centering function of a contract in the last chapter, but here I want to expand on that as part of safety as well. Like the cell membrane that holds and defines the cell, a contract places a frame around your work together, clarifying what will happen within the relationship container. That frame consists of an appointed time to begin and end a treatment or course of treatment, a discussion of what's needed, precautions to take, etc.

Usually a contract arises out of a request from a person to address some kind of problem they're having or a change they're seeking. It's like a cell membrane's receptors defining what that cell is needing or ready to do. Similarly, when we as practitioners inform our partners what we can and cannot do to address their problems—we're naming the receptors we're making available to the process. Clients feel safe when they know what will be done, how it will be done, for how long, what they might expect, etc. This may look like standard boundary setting, something that we've all learned about in our training, but the cell membrane model invites us to step into the complexity of that process with greater awareness and flexibility. The ongoing resonance and response between the receptors of healing partners in interspace often creates a rather muddy interspace that needs to be cleared up before safety can be restored.

The cell membrane must shift from moment-to-moment depending on what's happening in interspace, and fixed boundaries and contracts aren't often flexible enough to meet the demands. I recently facilitated a workshop in which experienced practitioners, all of whom were quite experienced boundary setters, were meeting to support each other in handling some of the challenging situations we find in bodywork. We discovered how difficult it is, once messages start flying in interspace, to be aware of what's being triggered in us, and to get a handle on what if anything needs to be clarified in the contract to help us move through the challenge. Simple boundary setting just doesn't work—it can create stiff, scripted phrases that function more as a reflection of our own anxiety than to create a healing response. The cell membrane offers a larger perspective, one in which we know that we and our healing partners are in this soup together, and both contribute to the safety or lack of safety we feel within the relationship container. Therefore, intention, self-awareness and clarity of contract work together to shape the quality of the relationship field, just like containment, selective permeability, interspace and oneness principles function in the cell membrane.

.

Informed Consent

The cell membrane also takes the standard practice of seeking informed consent into a more flexible and awareness building process. We all know that the more a client knows ahead of time about what will be done, when, and what will be expected of them that it helps them feel more safe. It also serves a protective function—the client can't sue you for doing something to which they've given consent, and you're prevented from engaging in anything risky they haven't agreed to. The cell membrane takes this basic idea a little further, in that the reciprocal nature of the relationship recognizes the importance of what both partners bring to the process. The one receiving treatment needs to know what's expected, how it might feel and the outcome possible, but the cell membrane model reminds us, moreover, that we're all in this together. We need to *cooperate* toward a successful outcome; it's not just what the practitioner does to another who has agreed to be done to. If we're following the cell membrane model, we know that both parties participate in the process and it becomes more than the patient simply agreeing to a procedure, once he has all the information about it. The cell membrane principles of interspace and Oneness inform us that whatever you do to me affects all of us. We all need to be aware of the opportunities and consequences of this treatment.

In Chapter 3, I told the story of how Dr. R. was seeking consent to more testing for Richard, the boy in the coma. The natural principles at work in both Dr. R. and Richard's mother took them into a dialogue in which they each became more aware of how their powerlessness to bring Richard out of the coma was affecting their decisions around further testing. Dr. R helped Julia become more aware of the factors contributing to her decisions, as well as his own by following the cell membrane model. They could then confer as equals for Richard's best interest. Our acknowledgment that Richard was still there guided us to communicate with him through interspace regarding his treatment. We never assumed he wasn't a part of the process, even though he couldn't directly grant or deny consent.

Standard informed consent practices only relate to what's clearly known about what's to happen. The cell membrane model informs us that as a procedure or relationship unfolds, unconscious material can come forward that also affects the decision-making process. I once worked with a woman with fibromyalgia who was very clear at the outset that she wanted only energy work—she didn't want to talk about "all that family stuff." Safe space for her meant space free of her "family stuff." I agreed to not inquire into family issues and continued to hold the intention for her overall healing. She was relieved to report that after just a couple of treatments she could walk around her house without pain. When, in subsequent sessions, her body started bringing up memories of "family stuff," she trusted that she was the one who brought it up, not me. Her receptors knew she was ready. We had her consent.

Natural Resilience in Safe Space

You begin to see that just about everything you and your healing partners do, say and feel contributes to the safety and sanctity of the healing space. Rather than paralyzing myself with over self-consciousness, however, I find that the cell membrane model, in and of itself, creates a safe space for me as I relate to others. By knowing that I'm not alone, but connected to a large web of relationships with other living things, I feel contained in a trust that even my mistakes

85

are part of something bigger than I can comprehend at that time. Within the cell membrane model, I know I will be jostled around by my mistakes, but that even those mistakes somehow serve some larger end, and my partners and I will grow from them. Angie comes quickly to mind.

I'd been working with Angie about a year when she called one morning, very upset. She and her college-aged daughter were at each other's throats, she said, and wondered if I had time to see the two of them together. I agreed to a joint session. I had worked with her daughter, Heather, a couple of times while she was on school breaks, but the more ongoing relationship was with Angie. Angie originally came to work on her outbursts of anger at co-workers and had been making great progress, but Heather was really pushing those anger buttons. During the session with both of them, I found myself really wanting to protect Heather from what felt like humiliating and derisive blasts from her mother. Try as I might to center myself, and hold the space safe for both of them, I just couldn't. I challenged and confronted Angie more than I usually did in an attempt to help her contain and be with her own anger and frustration, and not blast it out at Heather, who sat curled up in fear on the sofa looking like a defenseless kitten. They left a little more peaceful, but I could just feel the anger still simmering in Angie—now it was towards me, not Heather.

I couldn't easily dust the difficult session with Angie and Heather off my boots and move on. You might be thinking that it was my responsibility to protect Heather from her mother's blasts, to confront Angie about her behavior. Some therapeutic and relationship models do use confrontation as a tool. The cell membrane model, however, guides me to not take sides or try to rescue anyone, but facilitate balance in the system of which I was a part, to help Angie contain her rage without moving against her. The cell membrane also asks me to be conscious of which of my own receptors are active and contain my reaction to her rage. I reflected after the session on how my uncontained and unresolved feelings about maternal interference in a daughter's life muddied the relationship waters with Angie and Heather. My young adult memories of not being heard or understood by my mother were up for review. I knew what it felt like to have Mom judge me for being involved in politics or choosing a career path she didn't understand. I remembered how hard I tried, and sometimes failed, to be more understanding with my own daughter when she was that age. Now I'd failed to really support someone with whom I had slowly and carefully built a container of trust.

Angie cancelled our next session with a voice mail, so when I called her about re-scheduling, I really got an earful. Having supported and taken a little more of an edge off my own anxieties around mother/daughter conflicts, I was able to stay more centered in our call. She wanted to discontinue our treatment, saying she didn't think she could trust me again. After acknowledging how I'd reacted poorly, I invited her to come in for a closing session, for which she wouldn't have to pay. A week later she arrived looking bright and refreshed. She'd quit her job, bought a motor home and sold the home she hated, but had been holding on to "for her daughter's sake." In being forced to look at and listen to what her daughter was asking, she discovered her own unmet needs to strike out on a new career path—one different from the one in which she'd always felt trapped. After a year of traveling, she thought she'd have a better idea of what she wanted in this phase of her life. We talked about the mistakes I'd made in the session, how it hurt her. She accepted my apology, but also thanked me for the "kick in the ass." She insisted on paying me for the closing session. She called about six months later, saying she was having a wonderful time.

What does the cell membrane model say about my unconscious actions toward Angie, my attempts to force her into feeling the pain of what she was saying to her daughter? Often, differentiation in cells is triggered by some kind of stress in the environment, something that forces it to change. Even though Angie and I, each in our own way, dirtied the space we'd created, it may have been just the kind of environmental shift that forced Angie into a new evolutionary step. It doesn't excuse my unconsciousness or her cruelty to her daughter, nor does the cell membrane model encourage belligerence or carelessness just to create change. However, it can suggest that our behavior was responding to differentiating forces bigger than we were conscious of in the moment. The mother/daughter relationship receptors in each of us began to resonate in a way that

brought our process into sharper focus. Also, in a large, interconnected system with all life, we can't always know the bigger picture,
or how we are being influenced by factors in the larger holons of
which we are a part. Maybe the planets and stars were lined up in a
way that made us all more prone to conflict. Maybe, we were
responding to world anxiety and war, who knows? The only thing I
do know is that Angie, Heather and I ended up with more differentiated receptors around mother/daughter relationships. Angie took a
pretty creative stand for her life, Heather got her mother off her
back, and my power receptors got re-tuned. We, like all life, evolve
through challenge and resilience.

Physical Space

All of the non-physical elements of safe and sacred space I've been
describing become manifest in the physical space in which you do
your healing work. The kind of space you select for your work, and
what you bring into it reflects your intention and your awareness of
what's important to support healing. In addition to the obvious needs
to keep the space warm in winter and cool in summer, how does your
space let those inside know this is a container for healing? What
helps them feel safe as they enter? Do they have any contact with the
non-human-built environment, i.e. can they look out the window to
get a sense of where on earth they are, the time of day, what's growing this time of year? Physical space furnishes its colors, textures,
sounds and aromas to the healing space.

I remember hearing of a study years ago in which healthy
young football players were each placed in a bed in the intensive
care unit (ICU) of a hospital and simply subjected to the sights,
sounds, immobility and artificial light of the room without getting
any kind of treatment. Depending on the length of their stay, their
vital signs got increasingly less vital and they needed two days of
active life outside to recover for every day they spent in the ICU. All
that technology saves lives, but I can't help but wonder what the
space itself does to a vulnerable body. Like the cell membrane, the
designers of ICUs could be more selective about what is brought in

and eliminated from these spaces to enhance healing. I remain unconvinced that the flashing light and sounds of the evening news broadcast into a darkened ICU offers any benefit to the health of a severely compromised patient.

Just as the receptors on the membrane of a cell help to define what happens in that particular cell, how you create your physical healing space begins to define what you bring to the healing relationship, what you've chosen to put in interspace. The magazines in your rack or artifacts on your shelves can be chosen to welcome those you serve—ethnically, racially and culturally. Your space can reflect what is meaningful to you and your partners. A seasonal flower arrangement or care in choosing natural or full-spectrum artificial light for your space tells your clients that you are connected to nature's cycles, a connection you bring to the relationship you intend to form with them.

Draping and treatment garments

Another issue that relates to the physical space you create for your partners involves how you show your regard for your client's body, their container, by how you approach the issue of body covering. I remember feeling safe and cared for when the nurse in my gynecologist's office gave me a handmade gown of soft, colorful fabric to put on. I hadn't even met the doctor yet, and already this alternative to the stiff, cold paper gowns I was used to started this relationship off in a healing way.

In bodywork training, the attention paid to draping the client's body reflects the cell membrane principle of containment. There are specific lessons in how to wrap the sheet around the leg, for example, so that when you move the leg, the genitals remain covered. Or a way of placing a small towel over a woman's breasts to allow you to gently slide the sheet from under it to massage the belly. Clever and respectful, I thought, and realized that even these simple moves set the stage for the kind of relationship you establish with a client. What does how you maneuver the sheets say about how you are relating to the body on the table? I recall entering a massage room in which the sheets, a light blue, were placed on the table in such a way that I thought, "This person welcomes me." The upper corner of the top sheet was turned back softly and a candle was lit, inviting my body to its place of honor – another way of supporting my containment.

How much or how little to cover and how you do so is no small issue in developing the healing relationship. You want to offer protection and privacy, but also to avoid any implication that there's anything wrong with your partner's body. How you offer a treatment gown or manipulate the sheets carries the message to your partner's receptors of how you relate to the human body. A client recently expressed gratitude that I offered her a choice in draping, saying, "I just hate all that fussing and fidgeting with sheets—like something is wrong with my body peeking out!" Another feels safe covered in a sheet. The principle of selectivity helps you meet the body of your partner in a way that is safe and respectful, both by the message you send and what you're able to pick up from them in body language. If I sense that a practitioner is comfortable with my body in whatever shape it's in that day, it's easier for me to be comfortable with it. Interspace will be colored by your thoughts and feelings about looking at your partner's body.

When you work with dozens of patients in a day, it's easy to forget that when you pull up a sleeve to give an injection, or move a bed gown aside to get at a leg for a procedure, there's a body with feelings under that garment. Years of working with the human anatomy may make touching someone's body in places usually covered by clothing no big deal for you, but for someone sick or scared, the way you move the garment can make a big difference in the relationship development. I remember watching a hospice nurse roll up the sleeve of a man during his intake evaluation. She rolled up his sleeve as though it were a sacred garment, her fingers placed gently to hold each fold in reverence. She held his arm softly before wrapping it in the blood pressure cuff. That took a few extra seconds of her time, but she knew that time meant a lot to a man she wanted to help heal through death. The safe and sacred space for the relationship was set as she set his sleeve, something I didn't see in routine care.

Speaking of garments, what *you* choose to wear, sends a message into interspace as well, affecting the safety of the relationship space. Clothing reflects how you feel about your own body and also your sensitivity to your partner. How much does your clothing set you apart from your healing partners or help them feel like partners? Like receptors on a cell membrane, what does your clothing tell your partner about you? What aromas are you wafting into interspace? What do you ask from your partners? I remember a question from a student who asked what she should do about a massage client whose feet always smelled bad? I suggested she tell the client that she is sensitive to aromas (naming her own receptors) and that she finds it difficult to focus on the work when his feet smell badly to her. Would he mind washing them to make it easier for her to work with him? In co-creative healing relationships, remember, both partners are responsible for the quality of interspace.

Self-disclosure

In this and other chapters, I've stressed the importance of being very selective about what of your personal process you bring into the healing space with your partner. But sometimes, a client comes to you with a problem or illness that you, yourself, worked on extensively. It's difficult to decide how much of your experience with the same problem to share because it could either enhance or crowd the space your partner needs for healing.

Soon after I recovered from a surgery in which my uterus was removed—a procedure I tried to avoid for three years—a client came to me with uterine problems. I noticed immediately how much those receptors that hadn't quite gotten over the loss, wanted to jump in and tell this woman how awful it had been. Other receptors, however, could hear the fear and pain of the woman in a way that someone who hadn't experienced it may not have been able to. Having met at least that in myself, I could really listen to her, meet her where she was without asking her to take care of my loss. I chose to let those more healed receptors be the ones who spoke. "Yes, I had a similar problem, and although we're different, I have a sense of what you're going through." Feeling safe with someone who had an idea of what she was experiencing enabled her to enter her healing process with a little more confidence.

The resonance inherent in the selective permeability principle of the cell membrane model told me it was important to acknowledge that we shared a certain history, but asked me to be very selective about what I disclosed. I needed to choose what information to send into interspace based on what would help her, not take over her problem or shift her attention to me. Containment asks that you be able to tell the difference between her experience and yours, no matter how similar they initially seem. You're forming the relationship container for the purpose of her healing, to help her become more aware of her own process, not yours. I could attend to my remnant of grief later

Releasing too much of your own story into the healing space can distract your client from her own process. She may not need much of a nudge to allow her to escape from what's uncomfortable in her and focus on your story. She could also get the idea that you're more interested in what's happening with you than with her. Again, we return to the importance of intention—what is your intention when you self-disclose?

On the other hand, if you withhold your story when the experience you gained by living it can serve your partner, you might miss an opportunity for your client to feel less isolated. Since healing is a process by which we become aware of our interconnectedness, by carefully choosing what to share about my experience with my uterus, I helped my partner see her problem as one shared by others. Selectivity and Oneness work together.

Grounding

When you feel your ground, the ground of your being, you increase the chances that your clients will feel safe and you are more likely to act in accordance with the principles of your practice. Grounding is most simply about being anchored in your relationship with Earth, having your awareness anchored in your body as part of Earth. When I "accept the invitation of gravity," as David Abram, an ecologist and philosopher says, I feel more open to inspiration, to taking in whatever I need to support the work I'm doing. Like the prairie grass whose roots extend deep into the soil, I'm far more resilient to the storms my clients might be bringing to a session when I'm grounded. Likewise from a grounded place in my body my awareness can expand like leaves reaching for the light of the sun.

I imagine the kiva again. An elder or shaman is sitting on a rug on the ground of the protected space dedicated to healing. I'm coming to her because I've lost my ground somehow. I've been diagnosed with a serious illness, my life is in turmoil and mostly I feel like I've lost my way. The healer invites me to sit on the ground opposite her. As I approach her, I already feel her connection to Earth and can almost feel the root of her being penetrating the soil below, reaching for what will sustain her life. The light shining through the little *sipapu*, beams to the ground. I feel safe. Even though she may take me on an arduous journey, I feel like I can do anything asked of me.

The next time someone seems broken apart in your office or treatment space, try taking a moment to bring your breath to your feet and into the earth. When someone is angry with you or you feel anxious about what they're saying, feel the soles of your feet as they touch the floor. You may want to spend some time at the beginning of each day and at intervals throughout the day, just getting down. My writing mentor for this book, Hal Zina Bennett, suggests his triangulation exercise for grounding. You simply check out where your feet are and notice how far you are from two intersecting corners in the room, that is, where either the ceiling or the floor intersects with two walls. If you're outside, you can do this with trees or other solid objects. It gives you a felt sense of where you are. You could try an adaptation of this when you're locked in tension with a healing partner. Bring your awareness to your feet, then the feet of your partner and a third point a distance away from you for just a moment. Triangles are the most stable geometric form in nature, so when there's an imbalance between two poles (you and your healing partner), merely connecting to a third point can stabilize things. The Resources section of this book refers to books and training programs that can help you learn to ground and center, making it easier to offer that groundedness to your healing partners.

Inner sanctuary

The cell membrane principle of centering takes us to yet another dimension in our consideration of creating healing space—the safe and sacred space within each of us to which we can go during healing. When I help someone prepare for surgery or chemotherapy, I help them find that inner healing space, where through bringing forth their own images, they create a space where they feel safe and cared for. I ask others to imagine such a place before a session in which it's likely they will enter a traumatic memory. Peter Levine, the founder of the trauma healing modality called Somatic Experiencing, describes this as the "healing vortex" to which his clients are guided out of the "trauma vortex." This is not simply a mental construct imposed, like a band-aid, over something that hurts. Like an intention, it creates and/or taps into an energetic form that can literally transform the quality of the experience. Deep within all of us lies a pool of resources to draw upon when we need it.

Aquatic bodywork often takes people into non-ordinary states of consciousness where they enter an inner sanctuary. Whether they describe the space as deep in the ocean, within their mother's womb, or in the sky flying with eagles, within this inner sanctuary they often unwind pain, realign their bodies or gain insight into a troubled relationship. Your healing partner's inner sanctuary, like the DNA within the cell's interior, can then work with the part of them that meets the world, their personal membrane, to attract and transmit messages that enhance growth and healing.

Confidentiality

The cell membrane model adds another dimension to our understanding of the ethical principle of confidentiality. When we can view the relationship field as a safe and sacred container for a partnership in which healing is the intention, we're less likely to rupture that container by telling others about what happened there. Also, as we imagine our individual personal spaces and that of the relationship as both being selectively permeable, we know that what happens within one particular relationship container affects all others in interspace. The personal and relationship spaces are also affected by what happens outside. In other words, *we have to keep confidence within the container while also paying attention to the fact that we function within an interconnected web.*

Earlier, in Chapter 6, I talked about working within an interdisciplinary team with patients and their families. It was important that information got shared among patient, family and therapists, which left us in quite a few dilemmas when we considered the confidentiality ethic. As I reflect on one case in which I seemed to have managed that dilemma quite well, I realize the cell membrane model was at work.

The night before nine-year-old Brian's playground accident, which left him in a coma, his father informed his mother he was leaving her. But Brian hadn't been told about this. His parents came together to care for him, but after six months he suddenly woke up—the night after they again decided to split. It brought all of them back to our rehab team. As Brian began to communicate with me, spelling words on his alphabet board, he revealed intense anger towards his father. His parents wanted to know what Brian was telling me, while they tried to make plans around caring for him separately. His older sister had her concerns, and the rehab team was asking me for more information about his intense mood swings. Everyone had their own active receptors and intentions, so with all these interconnected relationships getting really sticky, decisions around confidentiality became a real challenge!

As I reflect on what worked to create safe space for all these relationships to evolve around Brian's healing, I see how the cell membrane principles offered the complexity and selectivity that a simple ethic of confidentiality didn't. What evolved may be of help to you in equally complex situations around confidentiality.

Start by supporting the primary relationship container.

The primary relationship was with Brian. Not only was he the "designated patient," he had obviously taken it upon himself unconsciously to manage the relationships within his family. Everything I've already gone into about the cell membrane's principle of containment applies here. Brian needed a safe and potent container in which to share his feelings, in the trust that I wouldn't tell the others. He didn't need his parents' emotional reactions to his feelings in that space just yet, or the projections of the other professionals on his team (selective permeability). He had the space then to really express, through gesture, sound, etc., the intense anger he felt towards Dad, and feel it supported.

Be selective in discussion with others.

Parents and team members always wanted to know what Brian was revealing in our sessions. I acknowledged their concern (supporting their container) and without giving details, said that he was slowly bringing a lot of complex feelings into his awareness and finding ways to express them, without giving details. Slowly, Brian himself began to express them to others, beginning with his nurse. In general I only told family and staff what they needed to know in order to do their work with him, like when they may need to let up a little on the work or give some extra support. Like the cell membrane, I was being selectively permeable between the membrane around Brian and me and that of the other members of the team.

Consciously expand the container when indicated.

When Brian began to open up to his nurse, he was expanding his own container, now that he felt better within his own space. Eventually, when the time seemed right, I suggested to Brian that we have a session with him and Dad together. He agreed. I met with Dad briefly first and asked him if he was ready to hear and receive what Brian had to say to him. Here, I was honoring the container I shared with Dad before expanding it to the three of us. It was painful to watch Brian haltingly point to the letters that told Dad how angry he was, and watch as he struggled to get his facial muscles to express the feelings. Dad really opened his receptors to Brian's feelings, and showed him so in many ways that Brian really felt. Interspace filled with the love they felt for each other, leaving all three of us in tears. You can see, I'm sure, how if I had just told Dad what Brian was feeling, the potency of Brian's anger and it's healing potential would have been diminished. If Brian's feelings had been bantered about the hospital, their power to heal would have been diluted.

What happens in one happens in all.

That meeting between Brian and Dad began a reconciliation that rippled through the whole family interspace, creating a safer large container for everyone. Brian's older sister began to talk to me about how her brother's accident and disability was affecting her. Mom and Dad were better able to plan how they would continue to co-parent after their divorce. Brian began to feel that he would continue to be loved and cared for even if his parents separated. Last I heard, Brian was still quite impaired physically, but his family was living well with the challenge.

I'm left with an awareness of how all the cell membrane principles work together to support confidentiality while also letting us know that the choices we make around it affect everyone involved and the healing space in which we meet one another. Confidentiality is often more than whether or not to reveal something, so with these tools we're better able to make conscious choices.

~~~~~

In summary then, the principles of the cell membrane offer both tools and context to help us create a kiva, a safe and sacred healing space for our healing partners. The elegant yet highly complex workings of the cell give us an equally elegant and complex picture of what it takes to create such a space. The relationship itself and the physical structure that holds it form the space, and both partners contribute to its quality through intention, self-awareness and clarity of contract. The physical space both reflects and grounds the healing intention, yet whether we're in an ideal, safe physical space or a war-torn village, we can awaken to the inner sanctuary in all of us that knows where the power of healing comes from. Let's go now to an exploration of the power to heal and what the cell membrane can tell us about managing power in relationships.

Chapter

11

POWER AND CONTROL
IN THE HEALING ARTS

Rivers and Tides, an inspiring documentary film about art, an artist and nature, helped me understand how we can work with power as we pursue the art of healing. In the film, Andy Goldsworthy, an environmental sculptor, follows nature's rhythms and contours as he creates his art out of leaves, pieces of ice, twigs and stones. It's as though I'm walking beside him when he wanders along the beach at low tide, gathering just the right rocks for one of his sculptures. He begins to fit one stone beside and on top of another. Sitting in my living room, I move into the energy of the stones, the sea and the spirit of this man. Each stone seems to say where it will fit—the artist, the rocks and the sea are all communicating—and I am there too.

Goldsworthy seeks to create a form that arises from the relationship he has with nature. As he carefully and precisely places each stone, he's acutely aware of the turning of the tide, soon to flow to the spot where he works. He and the stones together seem to know the sculpture's ultimate form. Sometimes the stones don't fit just right and he has to negotiate with them, chip a little here, a tiny wedge stone there, all the while looking back at the sea to check when it will soon be upon them. Holding the sculpture with one hand as he reaches for the next stone, he very gingerly places the new one where he thinks it might fit. Then click, another click, and the entire thing collapses!

He sighs, tugs on his beard, notes the rising tide and begins again. Stone by stone, a cone shape begins to appear. As I watch Goldsworthy's work take form, I am reminded of other similar shapes in nature: eggs, pine cones, seeds, tear drops. They too seem a part of the sculpture. At last the artist finishes and I watch, trans-fixed, as the tide seeps in through the rocks. Slowly the sculpture disappears into the sea. What strikes me so deeply, as I watch the sculpture vanish, is that the sea has carried with it this man's rela-tionship to place, his love for all he touches. In my mind's eye the crystalline form of the seawater holds the energy of this man, and that energy now affects the whole body of the Earth. As the tide ebbs, the sculpture slowly rises again, and I'm left wondering how many more waves it will take before it breaks and the stones again are strewn more randomly about the beach.

I want to touch my healing partners the way Goldsworthy touches stone—in humble awareness of where power resides in the art of healing. This film stays with me as I ponder what happens for me in healing sessions in which I find myself stuck, where the rocks have tumbled and the tide is rising. The parallels between Goldsworthy's art and the art of healing become clear as I realize that I, too watch, wait, listen, and observe the shifts and movement in my sessions. When I work with what each moment reveals, hold my intention and awareness as I let go of what I think needs to hap-pen, art unfolds and healing happens. Like Goldsworthy, we employ well-honed tools in the creation of our art. We develop skills and acquire knowledge, but it's only when we align those skills with the power of love, of intimacy with all life, that the art reveals itself. Like Andy Goldsworthy, we too must ultimately yield to an unfath-omable power, even the power of one unbalanced rock to make the whole thing collapse. Sometimes we need to surrender what we think is "our" art to the power of the tides to turn and reshape what-ever we think we're doing. I remember a session with Amber, a mul-tiply traumatized woman that went like that.

Amber and I had been working together for some time. While the events of this particular session were certainly not typical or even possible in most clinical settings, I include it here because it took me closer than most others to grasping the source of power in the art and mystery of healing.

On that particular day, Amber went into a deep grieving process during an energy work session. In previous sessions she usually had been able to enter and move through painful, intense emotions and come to a place of peace, or at least calm, within the usual time. As I applied one energy tool after another, like the sculptor selecting just the right stone to put in place, I looked at the clock to see that our time was almost up and we were nowhere near transforming this hunk of grief stuck in her body. I felt powerless to make anything happen before I had to not only end the session, but vacate the treatment room for the next shift. Amber's body shook and she could barely stand, much less walk alone to her retreat room. I may not know exactly what Goldsworthy felt as the pile of stones collapsed in front of him before the rising tide, but I have an idea!

I propped Amber in a chair and quickly changed the sheets on the treatment table for the next shift. I helped her walk to her room in the retreat center, helped her to bed and then my stomach growled in hunger. We both heard it. Hers was the last of five sessions I'd conducted that day, and most of them had been this intense. I was shot, hungry, and felt like a failure. I told her I would be back after I'd had something to eat and could recharge a little. I had to surrender first to the power of the tide within if I wanted to be of any help to her.

Forty-five minutes later, I found her curled up and shaking, apparently no better than when I left. As I went into my energy tool bag, I found it still empty. I went deeper inside, into my Center. All I heard was, "Just hold her." She nuzzled her way into my body, like an infant seeking a mother's comfort. Oh, this wasn't comfortable—not at all. I'm not her mother! And all this grief and need were triggering my own grief and longing receptors, which wasn't going to help! So I centered again . . . and again . . . and again, praying that some tool would emerge, something I can do that would help her move through this pain—and now mine! "Just hold her," is all I got. So I held her, doing my best to stay centered and calm my own grieving receptors. The grief she was experiencing had been locked in her body for many years, since she had been forced to watch pow-

101

erlessly as her three-year-old daughter was raped and tortured to death. No, I hadn't had that experience, but it sure triggered the times I felt powerless watching my own daughter in pain. I also had to watch other thoughts that arose from within, like "What do you really know about healing trauma anyway?" or "What are you doing in bed with a client, holding her like a baby? What if someone on staff saw you?" Everything I thought I knew about helping someone just fell to pieces, like Goldsworthy's stones.

The sun was beginning to sink behind the hills, but its last rays caught the silhouette of a large sycamore tree that stood outside Amber's window. The tree looked like a mother herself. Her trunk, the part visible through the window, bore two paired bulges just above a gentle, rounded bulge that made her look like the torso of a pregnant mother about four months along. If you know sycamores, they shed their outer layers year after year to reveal a smooth inner skin, one I always like to touch. In Kansas, they're whiter than the ones here in California and I always loved to see how they reflected the winter sun, standing as sculptures of nature to remind us of light in winter. Today, this weatherworn mother tree stood with us on that afternoon of grief. She drew me close to her as I sat holding Amber. I wondered, "Through how many storms has this tree stood as winds carried her leaves and balls of seeds away from here? What other forms of human suffering has she witnessed as people walked these hills on their pilgrimage to the healing waters?" In her presence I found it easier to just hold Amber.

Soon, both Amber and I were bathed in something I can only call the light of love. It was similar to the quality of love I felt as a mother, yet from a much less personal dimension. It came not from me, but through me, from what felt like everywhere. Amber softened in my arms, stopped crying and began to look around as though someone else had entered the room. The sky by now had created a swirl of pink and peach to bring out the black outline of the trees. We sat and watched in awe before getting up without speaking and walking to my car. Our hands touched and we stood looking at the sunset, unable to describe what we'd experienced, but knowing we'd been touched by the power of Divine Love.

Someone watching me go into Amber's room, climb into her bed and hold her, might have seen this as two people enmeshed in codependency—or worse. "Good therapists" contain the session within the allotted time and don't get into their clients' beds. But instead this was the cell membrane model at work. Let's look at the difference. You'll note that I had the presence of mind to take care of my own needs before attending to hers, even though her need was so pressing. In a codependent relationship her needs would have taken precedence over mine. I took time apart to feed myself (nutritionally and spiritually) before I could continue to work with Amber. I went to my Center, not only between the end of the regular session and when I went to her room, but several times during the work. Just as frequently, I noticed and contained my screaming receptors and asked for support.

Of course, Amber's childlike clinging to me indicated she was very much in transference, but I just let her need for a mother be in interspace. It was clear to me that I didn't need to be a mother right then—or even a great therapist. In codependency, each partner is awash in the other's emotional juices, indistinguishable from each other. One person eats cucumbers and the other one belches, so to speak. The cell membrane told me, however, that it was important for me to contain whatever emotions were rising in me, so that my feelings weren't flooding Amber's emotional field. I was able to differentiate Amber's experience from mine, which is impossible in the emotional fusion of co-dependency. Our subsequent work together demonstrated that each of our receptors, our response to grief and powerlessness, shifted and grew from the experience. By contrast, in codependency each partner reenergizes the wounded receptors of the other. The most important distinction, however, is that *we attributed the power to heal to our interconnection with all of life, the power of which we experienced as Divine Love.*

You certainly don't have to take a whole afternoon in a retreat center surrounded by lovely trees to experience the power and art of healing. It can happen suddenly at a person's bedside, in a moment of awakening during a counseling session or in a refugee camp. It's not the time or the place that creates the art, but a heart open to the power of healing.

Like the sculptor who watched his stones fall, the art of the session with Amber grew out of surrender. Amber, who had spent a lifetime mastering the art of holding on while her interior world was in chaos, for the first time really allowed herself to let go and fall apart. On some deep level, unknown to her at the time, she was ready to surrender the pain to a power greater than the grief and terror that gripped her body, just as Goldsworthy surrendered to the power of the tide. Even though I was accustomed to containing sessions within prescribed times and theoretical tools that usually helped Amber, I too had to surrender to something bigger than I could control. Often, in our work, when the rocks still lie in a pile and no tools are left to do anything about it, we're invited to surrender to a power greater than the apparent obstacles. That power resides in relationship—not a codependent, emotionally enmeshed one—but one that follows the model of living cells interconnected with all life. Trust in the power of differentiated interconnection, of separateness in Oneness, forms the context of such a relationship.

Looked at another way, Amber and I were like two cells whose interconnection made us aware of the source of our power to heal. Art works through and with Andy Goldsworthy and it worked through and with Amber and me. Goldsworthy has to hook up to the power of creation, the love flowing through nature's web, and so did we.

You may ask how I knew that this was a time to surrender my usual containment of therapeutic sessions to the scheduled time or space in order to follow this session to its natural completion. The answer lies in the way the cell membrane model guided me to check out and work with my receptors by paying attention to what I was feeling in the moment (containment and selective permeability). I contained and supported what was happening in me and connected to Center, from which I was guided to continue from an inner knowing that transcended the usual time limits. The growing trust in this process enabled me to "hook up" to the power to heal, instead of being caught in a web of emotions. Had I not cultivated a relationship to Center, not learned to trust when it said, "just hold her," a strict adherence to schedule or place could have limited rather than opened us to healing power. These decisions constitute the art of healing.

The technology and theories to which we ascribe the power of healing are merely tools in service to the power of love. When technology (or communication or theory) is used in love, we perform a healing art. As I watch Goldsworthy work, I feel his intimacy with the land and sea, his awareness that he is one with all of it, yet also separate as he shapes something within the One. There's no way I could imagine him smashing a cigarette, for example, on one of those stones, or throwing a gum wrapper into the river. Similarly when we align ourselves as practitioners with this power of love in the universe, the sense of interbeing as we work, we need not be concerned with misuse of power in our healing relationships.

But we aren't always conscious of this interbeing, are we? How do I explain the times I get frustrated with a client who seems stuck in a pattern and won't budge? The times I want to just shake someone's shoulders and tell them to wake up? Then there are the times when a client ascribes all kinds of power to me or expects me to soften years of their pent up tension. I find myself frustrated when clients don't do the self-healing exercises I suggest. And while it's not comfortable to admit, what about the times I just want to take the money and run? In these and countless other situations, the universal power of love doesn't seem to be there. You probably have your own list of power conflicts—times when you want to throw your power and authority at your client or duck from what they're throwing at you.

I'm talking about two dimensions of power here: the power of Universal Love that's always present and available (even when we're not aware of it) and the dimension of interpersonal power that we perceive as separate and limited in supply. Interpersonal power lies in the realm of duality; you either have power or you don't, or you quantify it somehow. If you don't feel you have much power, you want it, and those who have it want more or don't want to let it go. It's been assumed that in therapeutic relationships the practitioner has the power to both help and harm the client. That's why we have Codes of Ethics to protect the vulnerable patient from the powerful practitioner, to manage the unquestioned assumption of a fixed power differential in the relationship. No one questions that a surgeon with a scalpel can cure or kill, or that a social worker can either help or deeply wound a child in foster care. Even when we talk about empowering someone in healing, doesn't that imply that we think that person is lacking the power and we need to help her develop it?

Power and Polarity

I propose that nature would have us think differently about the power negotiations in healing relationships. Instead of the existence of a power differential, the presence or absence of a commodity in limited supply, nature would invite us to look at the natural shifts in polarity that occur everywhere in Earth. Let's look then, into how the cell membrane manages polarity, or shifts in power in relationships.

In my cell physiology studies, I learned how positive and negative ions (charged atoms or molecules) move back and forth across the cell membrane in order for the cell to do its work—a definite example of power shifts in nature. There's often a power differential, but it's always changing. In nerve cells, for example, it's that very movement from positive to negative and back again across the membrane that carries the nerve impulse along its path. Action is possible because of the polarity, but stops dead if the shift back and forth stops. So again, if you align your practices with how the cell membrane works, you would allow shifts in power back and forth between healing partners. Healing action is sustained when each partner alternately holds and surrenders power in continuous flow. No one gets stuck in either the powerful or vulnerable position, but gets more accustomed to both sides of the polarity and the ability to move with the flow. You may be doing that already, without knowing you were acting just like healthy nerve cells in relationship to each other. There's nothing inherently dysfunctional about duality in relationships; in fact it's essential to their formation.

If you believe that the power to influence change or healing in someone resides only in what *you* do, your healing relationship will falter. Within even the most involuntary or vulnerable healing partner the power exists to heal, especially in the presence of another who recognizes and can help them awaken to that power. The moment you allow yourself to experience power as flowing back and forth between you and your healing partner, the more available you both become to the higher, transpersonal dimension of power—which we call Universal Love. Andy Goldsworthy embraces the hard and the soft, the low tide and high tide, as he works. He accepts both his individual power to stack stones and the power of the sea to scatter them. And so it is with the healing relationship.

Looked at more directly in practice, I may possess the power to see or feel the energetic constrictions in someone's body and bring my hand there. However, I depend on the participation of my healing partner to be there too—even if it's only on a subconscious level. When both of us bring our awareness to the constriction, without trying to force anything to happen (the opposite of power), it begins to shift or release. The touch alone sometimes awakens a client to tension. "Oh, I didn't realize that was so tender," he says. Rather than using force to rub it out, I depend on the muscle to tell me just how close I can get. I need to listen; it needs to talk. Sometimes I see an image there with my inner eye, or sense an emotion. Before sharing what I find with my partner, I inquire first what he might be experiencing there. My purpose is not to show him the power of my intuition, but to invite him into an awareness of the power of what's happening in his body.

Throughout my career in hospital social work, private practice and energy work, I've observed that it's not just in intuitive bodywork that healing happens through a shifting back and forth of power. Gifted psychotherapists know the healing power of inquiry vs. interpretation. Physicians know that a patient who fully understands a procedure and participates in their own treatment planning is more likely to heal or encounter fewer problems of compliance with treatment. They engage the patient's power to heal. Yet, just yesterday a client told me that his physician said she thought it "unwise" to not pursue the treatment she was urging. We all get to the point where we have to take a stand for what we believe to be the best course of action, but how much more effective would it have been for the oncologist to say, "In 75% of people treated with this drug, the cancer is cured. I'd like to offer it to you." This way she states her case, but allows that there may be other factors involved in the patient's decision. She could avoid power-grasping phrases like "It would be unwise of you not to do this."

I get a clear reminder of the importance of being able to move back and forth along a power continuum, and fully accepting what we find at each end, when I do what's called "hot and colds" in the hot and cold springs where I work. It took me a while to get accustomed to stepping into very hot water up to my neck and then going a few steps to sink into the cold pool, and back again. Those experienced in the practice told me not to tighten up in resistance as I entered either pool, but just invite the hot or cold in. Take a breath and just feel it, they advised. The first time or two, I felt my skin alternately on fire, then sizzling like a branding iron being plunged into the cold water trough. After a few repetitions, however, all I felt was tingling skin and oh, so alive! In power struggles with healing partners we can find ourselves tensing up against either the heat of power or chill of powerlessness. What if you have an involuntary client, for example, who is only there because the court ordered him to be there? His physical body is there in response to the power of the judge, but he just sits there staring at you in defiance. Do you feel powerful or powerless? Imagine if, in such a situation, you don't resist the heat of his glare, just breathe into the feeling it evokes in you, and let the energy of his defiance sit in interspace. You fully accept the dance you're in along the power continuum, trusting that if you sit in powerlessness for awhile, something will shift —it's the way nature works with polarity. Maybe his clenched jaw softens, your eyes invite engagement—the stalemate is broken by your recognition of your involuntary client's power to do nothing and even his power to heal.

Pseudo-power

As I reflect on the power battles I had with my children when they were teenagers, I see that many of the issues were less about power, and more about the receptors that were firing among us around issues like self-confidence, alcohol, drugs and growing-up.

Similarly, power battles with healing partners can also be about receptors asking for attention. Much of our concern over abuse of power by health practitioners arises from conditions in which the practitioner is actually turning to a power play in order to leapfrog over their own sense of powerlessness—a condition I call pseudo-power. When we aren't aware of or fail to pay attention to the receptors that go off in our healing relationships, we're much more likely to exploit our clients for what is lacking in us. In the example above with the involuntary client, the therapist could have gotten real tough, maybe even aggressive, which would have just been a cover-up of his own powerlessness in the face of such a glare. The therapist wouldn't be aware of the differentiation principle working to awaken him to the healing potential of moving through his own powerlessness. I've witnessed nurses who insist on protocol, or force patients to get out of bed to go to therapy, who aren't aware of how exhausted they feel at having too many patients to care for in a system that doesn't listen to their needs. Therapists will sometimes set firm boundaries with their clients to avoid dealing with their own fear of getting too close.

When we subscribe to an inherent power differential between practitioners and clients, which fixes power in the practitioner, we can miss the power of the healing relationship itself to reveal what's ready for healing. When you stand with your partners in the light of healing energy, everything that blocks the healing gets illuminated. When you set the intention to be an agent for healing, you open yourself, maybe unconsciously, to invite these wounded receptors to come out of hiding, to open to the light of love. That session with Amber really showed me how much I often worked at making something happen with clients. All those thoughts and feelings that came forward about my inadequacy, the need to "do" more, weren't just standing in the way of healing, they *presented themselves for healing*. Rather than thinking something is "wrong" when you encounter issues of power in healing relationships, what would your healing relationships look like if you allowed yourself to be lovingly present with what comes forward between you? If professional ethics classes spent less time teaching how to control the power differential, and instead taught students how to attend to their own fears and doubts, students would be better prepared to work in alignment with the way nature handles power.

The Healing Power of Resistance

We're really taken to our power edge when we face our healing partner's noncompliance with medicine or an exercise regimen, cheating on diets, and all the other ways those in treatment sabotage their own well being. However, like the power of water rushing against rock, the turbulence that results when we hit resistance in our clients can also make the way for change. Resistance can drag us into control battles, tempt us into ethical misconduct—and—serve as a portal to healing.

The cell membrane helps me to understand that resistance is just one tough receptor, or set of receptors, that aren't going to budge until I meet them with awareness and compassion in interspace. Any time I push against them, try to make them move—in either my clients or me —the pressure goes up. Resistance, whether we bump into it in ourselves, or our healing partners, is kind of like a boundary; we think it's a barrier; we want to barge through it, maybe sometimes even knock it down. Resistance really gets our attention, and that's what it's supposed to do.

Lauren taught me quite a bit about the power of resistance. She appeared quite sure of herself as she asked me to participate in an interdisciplinary team she was assembling to treat her for leukemia. Impressed by the diversity and experience of the team she'd put together and the opportunity to learn more about the cutting edge research in more integrative approaches to healing cancer, I enthusiastically agreed. She had really done her homework on various modalities, and on me, it turned out.

Our initial contract was anything but clear. Lauren saw me as someone who could give her overall support through the healing process, which her research into the therapies she'd chosen had shown could be quite difficult. Even "natural" therapies involved some pain and fatigue, and she'd heard I was very caring. Yes, she knew I was a social worker and did energetic bodywork, so all of those skills would come in handy as well. My first mistake was not being more specific about what Lauren asked of me, other than using everything I knew to be of support.

Lauren asked for some bodywork to help calm her before her first meeting with the rest of the integrative healing team, especially the physician. No matter how I touched her, nothing was right. Too much pressure—could I lighten up a bit? Then, no, could I use a little more pressure? Later, in the team meeting, I watched her grill each of the practitioners, especially the physician, about their outcome studies, how they knew this and that. She really worked them over. They patiently tried to answer her questions, but it was clear no answer was good enough. Lauren's initial behavior as an empowered participant in her own care gradually revealed itself as a vehicle of resistance.

Some of the practitioners on the team resisted her resistance, told her this or that procedure was part of the protocol and she needed to agree to it. Others were bowled over by her belligerence and tried everything to please her. Lauren tried to get me to tell the physician what she wanted him to do, and for a time I thought I could support her best by trying to make peace between them. But nothing worked; her treatment program and therefore her life were at risk.

Finally, I'd had it. So many receptors were firing in me that I had to stop, seek the support of a friend and realize I didn't know how to help Lauren. From a centered position, I then told Lauren that I gave up; I really didn't know how to support her. It's obvious she wasn't feeling supported. I'd help her find someone else, I said, but really wondered what it was she was looking for. The diet wasn't right, the team members lacked compassion, the nurse didn't know how to draw blood, and that psychologist was really incompetent! How must it be, I asked, when everyone she so carefully assembled to help her was failing?

Standing with her in the realization of how everything was wrong, and by finally not trying to make it right, she got to the heart of her resistance. Lauren slowly revealed that her mother had died when she was a child, leaving her totally dependent on her heroin-addicted father. She used to watch in horror as he shot up, knowing she would soon be left alone for days at a time without any support from anyone. She had to learn to make sure she had what she needed when she needed it, yet no matter how much she tried to control her environment she always ended up being nasty, fearful and without support. Now, even her blood cells were failing her.

We worked on a new contract. She would let me know specifically what she needed for support and I would let her know clearly if it was something I could do. For example, she asked me to accompany her the next time she needed to have blood drawn. Intravenous puncture brought up understandable terror and fear of abandonment, so I agreed to stand beside her and help her move through the fear. We worked out a process with the nurse that involved giving Lauren more choice about the exact moment the needle went in while she held my hand. I'd remind her that she was safe through the quality of my touch or a soft whisper. This was one of many ways the use of power was made more conscious and brought more into balance in her relationship with the team. I wouldn't, for example, give *her* orders to the physician, but I would role play a dialogue with her around what *she* wanted to say to him, so that she could practice feeling her power without overpowering another. After a few such power-balancing interventions, she became less demanding and her treatment team began to look more competent to her.

Near the end of the treatment process, Lauren asked if I would just touch her spine as she lay on the table. I asked her to let me know, as I varied the pressure by increments, just which pressure felt good. Then I placed a hand where she asked for it to be, at the pressure we agreed upon, and she sunk into the presence of her own being. She was no longer ordering me around, and I was no longer either trying to suggest what had worked with others or running away from her. We'd reached a balance of power.

If you've been in health care for awhile, I'll bet you've encountered your own version of Lauren. Possibly those cases pop into mind as easily as those that went smoothly, maybe more so. You may have discovered that it doesn't work to force anything in healing. Lauren and others have helped me understand some basic approaches that foster healing in the face of resistance, which align quite well with the cell membrane model. In cells, action happens when there's a shift in polarity—giving and receiving, power and powerlessness. As you read the following, watch for how, by acting like cells in a balance of power, you can work with resistance and not against it.

Stop trying

The more you try, the greater the resistance. Even resisting the resistance is a form of trying. Trying harder doesn't awaken either you or your partner to what's really happening at your respective membranes or what's being fired back and forth in interspace. You continue to focus on your partner's behavior as she builds her defense against what you're sending. Even if you know that fear is supporting the resistance, you really don't have the power to make her fear go away by pushing at it with reasoned assurance, more things to try, or avoidance. Goldsworthy knew he couldn't either force the sculpture into shape or prevent the tide from changing what he created. He'd get bowled over if he tried.

Sometimes it's advisable to take a "step down" as you stop trying. You do this by consciously reducing your power in the impasse. Phrases like, "I guess I really don't understand," and "I don't seem to be getting this right," or "I'm confused," shift the power across the membrane to your partner, to provide just the impulse she needs to stop fighting. The stepping down has to be a genuine surrender, not just a verbal trick, in order for it to work. The energy of what you say gets heard through the words.

Clear the space

Pulling your awareness within your own container, to look at what receptors are firing, takes your anxiety out of interspace and begins to add safety to the space. If you go a step further than just containing the emotional energy and attend to your own charged receptors, then whatever has been cleared in you will enable compassion to flow into the space. When your need to fix, to make something better, or to enforce treatment fills the space, there's nothing for your partner to do but either run away or push back harder. No matter what you do, she may run away, but at least now with the space clear of your needs, you can begin to trust the power of healing instead of your force to bring her receptors more clearly into view.

Meet the resistance and the light will follow

When you meet the resistance with just the right amount of pressure and are willing to stay with what you find, resistance eventually yields to the power of the light. It doesn't matter whether you use the tool of touch, talk, instrument, your presence, or a blend of all these, you can bring a pressure to bear that just meets, but doesn't try to force, the tension offered by the resistance. In bodywork it can look like pressing in to the point where you feel the muscle begin to talk back, then back off a teensy bit and stay there awhile. In dialogue you can reflect back what you notice happening without the need to change it, letting the information rather than the force of your will influence the receptor of your partner. With strong emotion, I often just hold the feeling with my awareness and meet it with compassion.

With Lauren, I had to name what I felt happening between us (naming our receptors) and pull back my own emotional energy (containment). I went to a power source larger than my own ego (Oneness) to let go of my expectation of what she needed. By meeting her where she was, and backing off without distancing, the fear that locked her in resistance didn't have me and the other team members to focus on. Then, the fear was more available to the power of healing that could now move within and around us (interspace). We practice the *art* of healing in such situations. Once, while working with a young man who was convinced that he embodied evil, I had to meet the darkness in his eyes with just the right pressure of my gaze to invite the light to do its work, not unlike when I watched Goldsworthy hold a piece of ice at just the right pressure to complete the sculpture. The young man's dark gaze was so intense that I had to meet my own fear of evil with the same intensity of light. It seemed like forever, but eventually something lightened in him to create a shift.

As Eckhart Tolle says in *The New Earth*, "Nonresistance is the key to the greatest power in the universe," which can then emerge "as an all-encompassing Presence." By taking these three steps:

- Stop trying
- Clear the space, and
- Meet the resistance and the light will follow,

you can tap the potential of the resistance and avoid adding energy to the impasse.

Resistance isn't the only thing, however, that triggers powerlessness receptors—that feeling that no matter what you do, the one you're trying to help will just hurt anyway, maybe even die. These are the times when your trust in a healing power bigger than anything either of you can garner is tested.

The Power of Powerlessness

"I don't know how to help you," I said to Jolene. Deep despair wove itself into every thread of her being. She said it felt like there was a serpent of darkness slinking its way through and wrapping itself all around her, squeezing the life out of her. "It's helping just to be heard," she said, leaning away in shame ". . . and . . . that you're . . . h-h-ere." Jolene, usually a cheerful and sweet young woman, had surfaced some very painful memories of childhood abuse and ways in which she had hurt others as a result. We'd worked together for some time, and over the last year she'd learned some very effective strategies for releasing the energy of these traumas, but today nothing was working. The tool bag was empty again. As I sat beside her, I noticed that none of my self-doubt receptors were firing as they sometimes do in such situations; it was easy to stay in Center. I trusted that she would move through this pain, that light and love would come to her as it had so many times before for her. "This is a deep, core pattern now. As it releases," I assured both of us, "you'll be ready to grow even more." Our time ended with her still in despair, but able to be on her way. That is, I *thought* I trusted.

In the middle of the night I awakened with a nightmare in which no matter how hard I worked, I wasn't able to help a whole bunch of people in need. There were those *need to help others* receptors having their way with me again, asking to be honed a little more. One obstacle after another was thrown in my way in the dream, until I was nearly buried in a pile of stuff. It felt like Goldsworthy's stones had fallen on me, and I was helpless to move through them. I got up, did what I could to clear the energy and eventually went back to sleep.

The next morning I called my mother, now in full-blown Alzheimer's, only to hear her cry in rage and despair. She was inconsolable, so all I could do was just stand in the presence of her pain, knowing and accepting that I was powerless to change anything. Again, I was being guided by Center to do nothing and be love. How much helplessness could I stand in 24 hours? She was still crying, but saying I should hang up, so I did. I went to the forest, climbed the hill and gave my body to a big rock. The rock held me, much as the mother tree had years ago with Amber. The sun warmed me; Earth and Sky listened together as I cried. Tears of helplessness quickly passed into trust. A trust, deeper than what I had known the day before, took hold—Jolene will find her path and so will Mom. They will hurt again, and so will I, but there's a power to heal that is greater than even pain. It's the power of interconnection, of the natural flow of light to dark and back again, the power of divine love to ease the pain. Sometimes we only find it in our helplessness.

Suicide

For most of us who enter a health profession to help others, suicide presents the greatest relationship challenge—and demands that we clarify our relationship to power and control. I once asked my social work graduate students, in a course I taught on Loss and Grief, to imagine that they could live 500 years. While some of them pondered issues like overpopulation and the use of natural resources, most of them came to the conclusion that they would only want to live 500 years if they were healthy and happy. I then asked, "What if someone told you that you had to live that long in excruciating pain—either emotional or physical?" No answer—just blank stares for a while. "Well, of course not," they eventually mumbled, not realizing I was introducing them to our unit on suicide. This is how our suicidal clients see their lives—what feels like hundreds of years of relentless pain. What would the cell membrane model have us do in the face of suicide, and what can suicide and other life and death issues teach us about power and control in the healing relationship?

You may remember that in the first chapter, I mentioned that in nature, death is not a failure, but a transformational journey—a pathway to becoming something new. Within each cell lies the gene that determines the death of that cell. It's a necessary process to maintain the health of the whole, and it's the same in whole organisms as we recycle ourselves in the dance of life. When something in the environment signals to the cell membrane that it's time to go, that particular gene unfolds and death happens. The dance of life and death in nature is more complex than we can ever fully comprehend. In healing relationships, often the best we can do is help that dance be more conscious. We all have a "gene for death," a life process that will ultimately take us to death. For some, the wounds of life lead to thoughts of killing themselves. They can't see a way through the wounds, through the pain, and just don't want to feel it any more. Sometimes they want to rid their families or culture of what they see as their miserable presence. Suicidal clients (and those who seek assisted suicide) can take us to the edge of what we understand we're doing in healing.

Here's how the five-step process I described earlier helped me with Jolene when she wanted to kill herself—several times. Prior to our work as healing partners, Jolene had been hospitalized for other failed suicide attempts. Since then, each time she felt suicidal, I had to check out which of her many pain receptors were active and determine, in collaboration with her, the meaning of the messages she was sending into interspace. Was she asking for help? Wanting

117

me to know how much she was hurting? Did she have a plan? I checked out my own reactive receptors before deciding what message to send back. Was I afraid? What about those *need to help* receptors or the ones that feared making an assessment mistake that could result in her suicide? Should I take her to the hospital? If I did, would yet another hospitalization really help? And how would it affect the trust that tenuously held our healing relationship together? None of these questions were easy to answer, but taking myself through the process helped me understand the power dynamics at work. From a centered position I came to realize that even in those times when I took steps to reduce the chances that she could hurt herself, the power to kill herself, or not, was ultimately hers. By the time I had encountered Jolene, my receptors around loss, grief and suicide had been honed by years of experience working with dying patients in the hospital. I'd grappled with issues around assisted suicide and of course, exposed my receptors to lots of study in preparation for teaching the class on Loss and Grief. But, as healing partners often do, Jolene again took my receptors and me to the edge of what I thought I knew about my reaction to suicide.

One evening, Jolene called, not in desperation or despair at living, but to report on an insight she'd had. At the time, she was completing her nurse midwifery training and had discovered and begun to develop her healing gifts. Yet, in a moment of awakening, she felt sure she could better serve those in need (indeed, the planet itself) "from the other side," if she were dead. She wasn't on any kind of "high," wasn't wanting relief from pain or feeling shame; she didn't want any help other than to be heard as she talked through her ideas. She seriously wondered if her wounds were so great that the only way she could do the healing work she wanted to do was to exist beyond this wounded body. I checked out my receptors, and none were screaming in alarm. I connected to Center, from which I could just hold all of what she said in interspace and allow the time for her to hear them before responding. I asked questions that allowed her to examine her thoughts and feelings from different perspectives. When she talked about not wanting her family to suffer or for me to feel like I'd failed, I felt her compassion and also her resolve to live or die based on her life's path, not on others' need for her. She would write a letter to all those she loved, Jolene said, trusting that she could assure us that there was nothing we could do, we hadn't failed her, and that in fact we'd helped her get to the point of knowing what her life and possibly her death would be about. None of what she said, because she was so centered in her own understanding of her truth, seemed to knock me off Center or set off fear receptors. We expressed love and gratitude to each other and ended the call with neither of us knowing whether she would be alive in the morning.

I sat alone in the darkness of my living room, searching within. I imagined her killing herself, feeling the possible grief and sense of failure. I pondered whether her apparent calm and resolve was merely a mental program or a mask over her deep despair—the calm that often comes when someone is in a suicide trance. Richard Heckler, in *Waking Up Alive*, defines a suicide trance as that time when all a person can see, think or feel points them to suicide. In Center, I asked whether I should take some action; a responsible therapist takes action to prevent suicide. Yet, I couldn't act—nothing inside could support it. I went to sleep in peace, in surrender to the power of a woman to decide for herself whether to live or die, and why. I surrendered to the power of the tide, following its natural rhythm. How could I, after all, knowing the pain she lived with daily, take action to presumably take that choice away from her? I was prepared to live with the consequences of my inaction.

Heckler, in his sensitive and thoughtful book, points out that when someone enters a suicide trance, we're powerless to know exactly what will break the trance. The trance, which often outlasts the recovery from the suicide attempt, can be broken by kind, compassionate pleading or sometimes downright rude and cruel responses from others. Sometimes the trance is broken by something that awakens inside the individual—and the person decides to live. Heckler illustrated for me, years before that night, how, try as we might to control another's choice to live or die, we simply do not have that power.

Jolene didn't try to kill herself that night, but having the chance to explore it in the way she did took her through another labyrinth on her healing journey. She came through it with the knowledge that she chose life, and she said it was so important that I never tried to talk her out of it, that I trusted her to make the right decision, whatever it was. I felt a new level of trust take hold in the interspace of our relationship. The five-step process made the difference between the times I had intervened to prevent her suicide (and she was grateful I did) and the one time I didn't. In each instance, I thoroughly checked out both her receptors and mine and did what I could to help each of us connect to Center, the place that knows how to interpret what's happening at the membrane and decide on a healing response.

Of course, I don't actually know how I would have reacted if Jolene had killed herself. I suspect that after moving through all my emotional responses, I would find myself Centered in the trust that the power for her life ultimately rests in her and the web of relationships she shares with all life—in Oneness.

~~~~~~~

It's not my intention in this book to outline all the ways we can respond in a healing way to partners dealing with these major life or death questions, or get into the various philosophical, professional and legal perspectives on them. I simply want to say that when issues like suicide, assisted suicide, and treatment of the terminally ill find their way into your practice, that the cell membrane model can help you understand where the power lies. By connecting with your Center, it will be easier to know when to assert or surrender your power to influence whether someone lives or dies, and choose the most healing response. It can guide you to connect with the power within even a comatose patient or a pre-mature, severely impaired infant in order to participate in the decision around living or dying.

Walter Cronkite used to end his nightly news broadcast with, "And that's the way it is." His voice lent a sense of acceptance to the daily news, a trust in a power greater than the stories he reported. Something in me often says the same thing. We use our medicine, touch or ability to say just the right thing, and these tools often help a lot. But sometimes nothing works, and then our healing relationship depends a lot on our relationship with power and control—our ability to engage in the art of healing. At those times, the cell membrane can guide our response in such a way that we draw the power of Love into the relationship and not try to control one another. The former Beatle, George Harrison, wrote lyrics about being down upon his knees, looking for his life as he faced death from cancer. From down on his knees he found his way to Love— the ultimate power to heal—and so can we.

~~~~~~

I'm going to shift the focus here for a bit to introduce a broader perspective on the issue of power. Sometimes, no matter what we do in our individual practice, or how motivated our partner is, there are forces at work in the larger community that send us either into another kind of powerlessness or a feeling of isolation. What does it matter, for example, if you and your partner agree on a course of treatment, but the insurance company doesn't think it's "medically necessary?" What if you're a practitioner of a modality not recognized by the conventional medical system, and your healing partner's physician is advising against working with you? Or conversely, you do what you can to help someone medically and an herbalist suggests a compound that interferes with the action of the drug you've prescribed? If the diet you recommend goes against the cultural values of your partner's family, how do you reconcile that? You may know that organic food reduces the toxicity your partner is dealing with, but they either don't have the money to buy it or can't travel across town to shop for it? What if you schedule surgery for a certain date and your patient says the moon is in the wrong phase on that day? How do war and terrorism find their way into your healing space?

Power and Integral Healing

Power struggles aren't confined to the relationship between individual healing partners. Our professions are at war too. It may be a subtle war, but the helping professions do what they can to influence the health consumer to believe that their particular approach carries more power to heal. There are licensing boards in many states that grant the power to use the word "healing" to a select few of all those who practice the art. Where I live, people hesitate to say their back hurts, or that they have a headache, to avoid the barrage of suggestions from those in possession of the most powerful herb, homeopathic remedy, or bodywork modality for their pain. Conventional medical practitioners accept some complementary and alternative approaches, but view them only as supplemental to what *really* is proven effective. Some new age warriors treat someone taking an antibiotic or submitting to surgery as a defector from the cause.

An emerging paradigm, called integral healing, takes us to an understanding of the power to heal that aligns itself well with the cell membrane principles. Integral healing begins with the awareness that the power to heal arises through the interconnected web of relationships with all life—the inner and outer, the scientific and spiritual, the objective and subjective. It includes allopathic and homeopathic, individual and family, society and natural environment, all in relationship to one another. Practitioners of integral healing know that the power to heal isn't concentrated in one individual, technology or approach to healing but flows through all disciplines that authentically and heartfully dedicate themselves to healing. As Ken Wilber says in the Foreword to the book, *Consciousness and Healing*, "No one approach is 100% wrong."

I envision a health system where conventional medical practitioners embrace complementary and alternative healers as equal partners in the art of healing. In this system the boundaries between them fade to reveal relationships in which separate skills are recognized as differentiated partnerships arise. The energy healer would work beside the oncologist to administer chemotherapy that carried light medicine to the cells, along with the chemicals. With an acceptance that wherever we touch the planet, we're touching all, many of our dilemmas about whether it's best to focus our action on cleaning up the toxins in the environment or helping people detoxify their bodies would lose their potency. Integral healers understand that partnerships among all who dedicate themselves to healing will forge the way toward developing the consciousness needed to create community and global healing. We're all in this together.

The integral practitioner develops her awareness of everything being connected to everything else even as she specializes in one particular healing practice. She doesn't rest her confidence on only one approach, because she knows she must address various dimensions of the problem to meet her patients' needs. That doesn't mean a surgeon has to know how to help someone with the family issues that impact a patient's healing, but she should recognize their importance. An integral dietitian understands the soul wounds of someone suffering from anorexia, even if she, herself, is working only on the nutritional aspect of the problem. Integral healers recognize the impact of other dimensions of being on the healing processes of their clients. They understand that each healing partnership stands within the larger web of partnerships and that the web itself is a source of support.

Another way of looking at it would be to visualize the client/practitioner relationship as being in the center of a series of concentric circles, each representing a field of influence that exerts its power on the healing relationship. Figure 6 shows the power map for someone coming to you with digestive problems, for example. Power flows back and forth across the spheres of influence, thereby creating an open, interconnected system.

Power moves all around this self-organizing, co-evolving, living system that influences individual health. Wherever you work, whatever point you touch on this circle, you affect the healing outcome. Conventional paradigms, which place the locus of control (power) for healing solely on the practitioner or the practitioner/ client relationship, fail to recognize the power of the other spheres of influence on this one person's digestive system. Individual nutrition is influenced profoundly by how safe the food is, the emotional

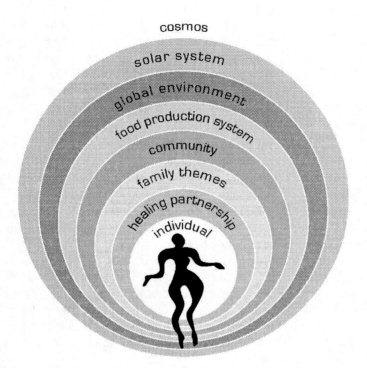

Figure 6. Power and Control in Integral Healing: Interactive spheres of influence on the healing process of someone with digestive problems. From inner to outer spheres:

- individual with digestive imbalance
- therapist with skills to treat imbalance
- family themes of both healing partners around food
- community values and means to make healthy food available
- health of food production systems, soil/water quality, transportation
- economic and political systems of control
- global environmental health
- solar system activity
- cosmic energy

environment in which it's eaten, and what that person's experience of nurture has been on physical and emotional levels. In my immigrant family, for example, food was equated with love and you showed Mom you loved her by eating her food. My parents reached their teens during the Depression, so when I made a face at meat and went straight for the green beans, my father took that as an assault on his ability to finally bring home the bacon. As I grew up, tended my own garden, and learned about all the political, economic, global and cosmic influences that come to bear on what I take in, my understanding of nutrition expanded immensely. Someone who tries to help me with a digestive problem would be best advised to know that we're doing our healing work within this web of influence and that the outcome depends on all of these. That's not to say we try to exert power at all of these levels at once. It's more like when we're driving a car, our peripheral vision takes in the whole scene around us, while we focus on the pedals and steering wheel. It's helpful to see, however, that the car in front of us is turning left or that a storm is brewing, as well as the signs that tell us what each gas station is charging today.

~~~~~~~

Like Andy Goldsworthy, who shapes his art in mindful awareness and spiritual intimacy with the land, the sea and the rocks, our sense of power and understanding of what we're doing in the healing arts can be shaped by an awareness of the intimacy of the web we share with all life. It changes our sense of responsibility, and therefore power, to realize that we're not alone in treating someone; the outcome doesn't depend entirely on us. At the same time, we know that if we abuse our power in healing, we are hurting more than one person, we are hurting the whole, including ourselves.

This expanded idea of where the power lies in a healing relationship can help you to:

- place your ideas of who's right and who's wrong in a larger context when you find yourself in a power struggle with your client or other healing professionals

- recognize that more is involved in any particular healing challenge than what you can accomplish alone
- connect with a greater source of power when you feel powerless to help someone
- work consciously with the power of Love in the universe

Another way power shows up in healing relationships is through money—the vehicle of power created by modern human culture. As you can imagine by now, the cell membrane has something to offer us again, as nature's model for power and resource management.

Chapter
12

MONEY AND THE HEALING RELATIONSHIP

Most people enter the healing professions motivated by a sincere intent to make a positive difference in people's lives. While money may not be what motivates us, and many of us are even uncomfortable talking about it, our feelings about money, like all the other influences that have shaped us, inevitably enter into our healing relationships. Wounded money receptors, the ones that got formed in fears about security, scarcity and self-worth, will block our best healing efforts if left unattended. The more conscious we are of the money issues we and our partners carry with us into the healing space, the more we can foster healing instead of harm.

When we choose to practice more holistically, more in alignment with nature, we must come to terms with the role money plays in the holistic paradigm. We can no longer deny that issues around money have been having their way with our relationship receptors all through our lives. Our clients walk through the door with them, and skillful practitioners work with these issues in ways that serve healing intent. The cell membrane can help us and our clients bring greater awareness to how the exchange of resources can in itself become integral to the healing process. To illustrate this, I'd like to start with a couple of case examples.

Tom's Healing Pilgrimage

Tom came regularly for energywork with me, during which he not only experienced relief from chronic pain, but also transformed layers of trauma from childhood. In each session he would courageously enter and meet those places of terror and together we would witness them yield to the power of healing light. Some of his sessions were excruciating, but by moving through the trauma and transforming it, he was achieving levels of functioning he'd previously thought were unreachable. For me, these sessions were exceptionally co-creative, often drawing more resources through me than I thought were there. He discovered his capacity for healing and hope, and I developed my healing gifts in more ways than I could have imagined possible. We never talked about money, but I couldn't help but wonder how he could afford to come to this retreat center so regularly and pay for sessions without having a job. After several months, he told me, with much shame and regret, that he wouldn't be able to come anymore because he was living on a disability income and had hit his credit card limit. It was then that I realized how money had been in interspace all the time.

Tom didn't think much of himself, was even ashamed to be the person he thought he was. Being able to pay me was the only way he could justify the treatment that he knew held the potential for freeing him from his inner terror. He turned away, not wanting to face me when I suggested that we write a proposal to the retreat center for discounted sessions. There was no way he could do it, he said. I thought then about the nature of this place where I work, the sacred energies that have been calling pilgrims here for centuries. I told Tom that I believed by tapping into these resources, he gave the healing energies here the opportunity for expression, a chance to be received. The retreat center and I serve this larger purpose, I said. It took him quite a while to consent to asking. When the manager brought us a credit voucher later that week, a gift from the retreat center for Tom's healing, we all felt like we'd experienced nature's way of managing resources for healing. Tom and I, the retreat center management, and the land and water, like cells interacting with each other through interspace in a holistic system, all brought the best we had to the process and we all benefited from the exchange.

Lucy's Path

Lucy worked in the fast lane, making lots of money manipulating people and real estate. She'd come to the retreat center often for bodywork to release the tension in her body and she really liked my work. She gave me large tips (tipping is a normal part of the compensation here) and always asked for work in the same part of her back. Her schedule was tight also, so she often asked if I would come in on my day off, or at a time when I wasn't on the schedule. She tickled a lot of my receptors, for sure. I liked her and she was very responsive to the work, but I began to feel more like a servant than a healing partner. Was I just like another piece of real estate she bartered for? Plus, I was getting really tired of being the one responsible for working out the kinks and pains she created through her high-intensity lifestyle. I sensed deeper issues within that muscle tissue that might take her into greater awareness of what her body was trying to tell her. I began to notice a slight sinking feeling when I saw her name on my schedule, and a bit of frustration while working on her back. My best skills for helping someone move into deeper areas of healing were not being utilized. I was making money, but not being paid—you know what I mean? There was no balance in either resources or responsibility in the exchange between us. Neither of us really grew from the exchange, and our respective attitudes about money weren't helping. She worked hard for the money that gave her the power to acquire what she wanted, and I felt like one of her acquisitions. Before we go further with how I resolved this problem with Lucy, and how Tom and I continue to work through issues with money to foster his healing, let's look at how the cell membrane gives me clues how to respond to each of them in a healing way.

Cells and Money

You won't find cash flowing in interspace between cells. Money is something humans created as a medium of exchange for goods and services. Lynne Twist, author of *The Soul of Money* says:

> *"Like water, money is a carrier. It can carry blessed energy, possibility, and intention, or it can carry control, domination, and guilt. It can be a current or currency of love—a conduit for commitment—or a carrier of hurt or harm."*

Boy! That really struck a cord in me when I heard Lynne say that in a workshop. To think of money like water, sounded to me like the energy that flows throughout living systems that live in balance and harmony. The flow of nutrients, water and energetic information among all cells in the body sustains cellular relationships. If we appreciate money as a current that flows through our healing relationships, how will that affect how we work with money in the relationship? I reflected then on what is being carried by the exchange of resources between my clients and me, and what living cells can tell me about how to relate more skillfully with them around money. Since the cell membrane manages the flow of energy in cells using all the principles we've been talking about, a closer look into how cells do this could be helpful:

Flow-through Systems

Nature is a flow-through energy system, managed by the receptor molecules in the cell membrane, with currency moving in a balanced way among all the tissues in the body. Your healing partner is like a cell that needs something from another cell—you. Your partner, however, has something you need—money to pay your bills or an opportunity to apply your healing art. You both benefit from the flow of resources between you. Cell membranes, like healing partners, draw what they need from interspace and release what's needed by other cells to benefit each other and the system of which they are a part. When there's a blockage in this flow, illness ensues. In healing relationships a lack of flow can block the healing process. You may recognize the similarity between these flow-through systems and the balance of power relationships we explored in the last chapter.

As a flow-through relationship system, both healing partners give and receive something of value that helps sustain not only the individuals in that relationship, but also all others with whom we're connected. By accepting our grant to help with the cost of healing sessions, Tom gave both the retreat center and me an opportunity to be more conscious of this flow-through, to align us with the Oneness and interspace principles, both in dollars and in commitment to a purpose. His acceptance helped me to create an equitable balance of give and take in which we all felt served with what we needed. Lucy and I were each blocked a bit by our attitudes toward money, and even though money was being given and received, it didn't feel in alignment with nature's way with relationship.

Collaboration

The flow-through system is managed by the selective permeability and differentiation of the cell membrane in collaboration with the nucleus (center) and other structures within the cell. Cells work together, each with a different job, to effectively and efficiently sustain the organism of which they're a part. The cell membrane, as the main message communicator, responds to the vibrational messages it picks up from other cells to signal the structures inside the cell on what to do next. At the organ level, even though the brain and other parts of the nervous system may appear to be in charge, the brain's currency, its very existence, depends on the collaborative work of all the other organs. The final result is that more overall resources are available to the plant or animal when the cells work together. Without that kind of collaborative effort, evolution wouldn't have moved far beyond the single-celled organism.

Tom, the retreat center management, and I collaborated with the natural resources at work here for healing. The current running through our resources carried our intent, and by directly bringing our awareness to money, we became even more conscious of the sufficiency within which we were living and working. A more enlivened healing energy began to flow through our sessions.

Initially with Lucy, there was little sense of collaboration in a true partnership. Our relationship was one in which the boundaries were strictly defined as practitioner and client. Even though Lucy paid me money for my time and expertise, I didn't feel her participation in the healing process beyond that. When I began to invite her awareness more into her body, not just allowing her to drift off into unconsciousness, she willingly became more engaged in her own process. I felt my resources being tapped in service, no longer like a servant. Yet, differentiating shifts like this can bring other receptors into awareness, as is the way with differentiation in cells and healing partners. I heard one receptor saying, "Watch it, you might be risking a good paying client!" Following the five-step process, I tracked, contained and supported that fearful receptor around money and then connected to Center, where I could link with my healing intent to involve both partners in co-creative healing. Once we stood on more balanced footing in the collaboration, with Lucy more active in her own healing process, she was surprised to discover resource-depleted places in her body. Her back was lacking support in ways no money could buy and she began to look for ways to bring a different kind of currency to her body. This leads us to another aspect of portfolio management in cells.

Distribution of Resources and Responsibility

Among cells in a healthy system, resources are distributed according to both need and a particular cell's responsibility for the system. Every cell has enough to do its job, even though it gets more or less food or oxygen than other cells. The brain and its cells, for example, get a lot of oxygen because, relative to other organs, the brain carries a greater responsibility to the whole organism. The bone cells, however, don't suffer from this distribution pattern; they get just what they need to hold us up. We could live if we lost a bone or two, but without a brain, the organism soon dies. In brain and bone, both "agree" that the distribution of resources is correlated to the level of responsibility each has for the health of the whole system, and each gets what it needs.

We have to look beyond two individuals, or even the healing team, to understand how the way money is distributed and responsibility for care is allocated in modern healthcare systems affects our healing relationships. The resources available to us as practitioners, and to those we serve, often depend on those outside the direct relationship. Most of the money often goes to those least responsible for what actually happens in healing. Large amounts of money go to pharmaceutical and technology providers and institutions that never see or touch the person in need, although they provide important structural components to the healing, just like bones do. Decisions for what treatment is performed, and for how long, are often out of the hands of the patient and practitioner, centered in the protocol books of the insurance companies. Who gets insurance and at what cost depends on factors far removed from the healing relationship. It's a large, interconnected, collaborative system alright, with money flowing through it, but the distribution of resources isn't going to those most directly responsible for the healing—you and the person who comes to you for help. The structures of the healthcare system need resources, of course, but like the bones in the body, they carry less of a responsibility for what happens in healing than do, say the heart or immune system—or you and your partners.

How you respond to these systemic limitations in resource allocation can affect your relationship to your work and to your healing partner. By knowing how nature facilitates the flow and distribution of its currency, you and your partner can work creatively to bring both the distribution of resources and responsibility for healing more in line with nature's balance.

Tom isn't valued in a culture that values commercial productivity; Lucy is. They each brought that cultural value into our work together, and that cultural value affected the healing relation-

ship. I couldn't change the culture to make my work more in alignment with nature's principles, but I could work with the resources I
had to make a difference in the healing relationship. I valued the
resources Tom brought into our relationship: courage, motivation,
money he could afford, and a willingness to tap into inner resources
for his own healing. He also helped the retreat center and me tap into
our resources to keep everything in flow.

Lucy didn't know she had any resources other than money
to affect her own health. Her money was being distributed in a way
that drew her out of responsibility for her back tension. I was taking
her money, but not taking responsibility for the resources I had available to her healing. When I gently confronted her about the fact that
she came in for the same work over and over, and she consciously
agreed to look more deeply into what her back was wanting to tell
her, it brought both of our resources into a more balanced distribution and responsibility.

The situations with Tom and Lucy illustrate some of the
many ways money makes its way into our healing relationships. You
probably have examples of your own where something about money
stood large in your healing space, but until something felt uncomfortable, you or your partner weren't aware that it was there all the
time. You possibly didn't know what to say or how to respond; we
don't talk about money much in our training programs, and even
when it shows up in ethics instruction we only know we aren't to
exploit our partners for our own monetary gain. That's not what it's
about, is it? The examples below are more what I hear from practitioners. Maybe some of these come from you:

- You're working harder or longer than is healthy for you,
  because you need the money.

- Your healing partner wonders how much longer she can
  afford the care you give, and begins to hold back in her
  treatment.

- You want to charge a client for missed appointments, but
  you're afraid you'll lose him as a client.

- Your patient's receptors pick up the message that you only have seven minutes to spend with her, so she doesn't bring up what's really bothering her.

- You hesitate to refer someone to another therapist because you fear the loss of income.

- When you're worried about making ends meet, you may hesitate to challenge the guy who isn't fully participating in his care or expecting you to fix him.

- You find yourself giving someone extra special treatment if s/he can benefit you financially in some way.

- The insurance company won't authorize treatment that you and your healing partner think is necessary.

- You don't take time for continuing education or rest and renewal because you can't afford it.

- You stay with a "safe" job, rather than following your calling to work in a different setting or modality.

Making Nature Your Money Manager

You may be feeling that you have no power over these situations. Maybe you work in a system that determines how many people you work with and what you're allowed to do with them. If you're in a private or group practice the insurance company may be the third partner with whom you and your patient must collaborate. We've all downloaded our culture's messages about money and they gnaw at us when we feel stressed or undervalued. Lynne Twist helped me see that most of us participate in the cultural myths of:

- *There's not enough (money, time, love, etc.)*
- *More is better*
- *That's the way it is*

The sense of powerlessness that stems from these myths can affect our ability to follow the calling that initially led us into health care. It can keep our clients and us in fear and helplessness, preventing us from seeing the resources that are available to make a change. The living cells in our own bodies, however, can teach us how to meet these myths with an awareness of sufficiency. We may not be able to overhaul our entire health care system just yet, but in our own settings and treatment spaces we can contribute to a shift towards the cellular way of managing our resource portfolios. In offering the following suggestions for you to consider, I invite you to explore how they might be applied in your setting.

Intend to notice and care for the receptors activated in you and your partner around the resources you each bring to the treatment.

The situations listed above and those you find coming up in your healing relationships awaken you to which messages or myths about money are active in your emotional field and that of your partner at any given time. With Tom, for example, bringing up the issue of money gave us the chance to work with the receptors he'd formed around shame. With Lucy, I got to examine my attitudes about being a servant vs. being of service. It's important to remember that awareness of what's happening is the first step toward shifting the hold that money messages have on you and your partner.

Examine what sufficiency means to you.

No matter how many clients, or how much time and money you have, somewhere in there you'll find a feeling of sufficiency. Bones and brains each need a sufficient amount of energy to do their respective jobs for the body, even though they use vastly different amounts of energy doing so. *Sufficiency is a measure of the quantity and quality of resource flow that allows you to do what you're called to do.* How much money will it take to allow you to stay in practice? How much time with family or in continuing education will keep your energy flow in balance? Is more time with your patients really what's needed, or can your undivided attention and compassion enable you to do more in the time you have?

136

I don't pretend that maintaining a sense of sufficiency is an easy task or that once it's done, it's done. You can look for signs from the receptors in your body, for example. For me, when no one signs up to work with me, the receptors that say I need a rest have a chance to speak up. At such times I ask myself questions such as the following: Am I feeling unappreciated in my work, or working hard for little compensation (money or satisfaction)? What would it take to come to a sense of sufficiency? A different kind of work? A higher fee or salary? Pay attention to the signals that play into the toxic myths Twist refers to and notice if you're reacting to those myths or responding from your Center with an inner knowing of sufficiency or lack thereof.

The idea of sufficiency can also come up in those situations where either you or your client fears she's becoming dependent on you. This isn't about money, per se, but it does relate to sufficiency in an emotional way. Exploring sufficiency together can lead to growth and a sense of sufficiency in both of you. For example, Linda had times of intense anxiety, when just knowing she could check in with me by phone helps to calm her. Previous therapists had limited her to a specific number of calls at specific times during a week for 10 minutes or less. If something came up at another time, she had to deal with it alone. Strict boundaries such as this only added to her internal pressure, fear of abandonment and low self-worth. Linda found that she organized her life around those specific times and therefore felt even more dependent on the therapist—something neither of them wanted.

We worked out an arrangement where, when she wanted to call me, she checked within to see if her inner resources were sufficient to calm the anxiety. When she called, I trusted she'd tried what she could and that if it isn't a good time for me, I will tell her so and we would set a time for another call. Admittedly, this was difficult for me at times, times when I felt I needed some space, or was played out for the day, but was concerned that if I said so, she'd feel abandoned. Yet that too gave me a chance to dialogue with my own receptors around sufficiency and dependency. However, Linda came to trust that when I was there, I was really there, and that meant a lot to her.

137

We worked out and changed our arrangement over time, which required that we both be more aware of what we thought was sufficient support and personal space. While it wasn't always easy, it eventually led to more trust rather than a power dynamic. This process allowed for the flexibility one would expect from a living cell in which membrane receptors grow and shift in response to what's happening in their relationship to other cells and their environment.

If you find yourself becoming dependent on a healing partner, financially or emotionally, you can, of course, take yourself through the inner work necessary to identify which receptors around sufficiency are acting up. I deal with these concerns in more detail in the next chapter on Dual Relationships.

Jointly assess the value of the healing partnership.

I've just begun to experiment with *value-based* rather than time-based or "what the traffic will bear" approaches to fee setting. Most people in private practice charge by the hour or minutes of contact and the rate is determined by standards in the profession or what is usual for what you do and where you do it. I recently paid $93 for a 10-minute consultation with a nurse practitioner about a bladder infection, but paid a massage therapist $75 for an hour of exquisite work on my neck and shoulders. You may be thinking that the nurse practitioner has more years of education and experience, but that wasn't the case. Both treatments were of value to me, but 10 minutes of asking a few questions and writing a prescription carries less value to me than an hour of skilled and focused work. For you, the value may differ.

With several of my regular clients, we negotiate a monthly fee that reflects the value of our work together. In that negotiation, we consider what services (treatments, phone and email consultations, meditation support, etc.) from me are indicated based on her situation and what she will provide (money, commitment, homework assignments, etc.). This kind of direct attention to value was initially difficult for me and for them, but we soon found that we liked not having to count every minute and compute every dollar. I'm encouraged by the process to consider how I value the work I do, and my healing partners get to compare the value they place on their healing compared to other things they spend money on. Sure, the usual professional standard enters the considerations, but so does how much the client can afford, and the level of participation and commitment we're asking of each other. A dollar value for the services we agree upon often arises out of interspace after we sit in contemplation asking for what is a sufficient amount—and most often it feels right to both of us. We place money right in there with the other energies we bring to the healing space. By doing so, we bring greater clarity to the resources we exchange in our work, and the money carries the current of our intent. It's important that both of us feel comfortable about the monetary value chosen; neither one feels exploited or over-stretched—we work within a sense of sufficiency.

My clients and I notice that this kind of fee-setting system acknowledges that the value is in the relationship, not just in what we do during scheduled sessions. The benefits of the relationship extend to the times between sessions when my partner practices self-healing exercises, or "hears me talking" when she has a question in her mind. If I know she's undergoing a diagnostic procedure that day, I'll spend time linking with her in meditation or sending supportive energy her way. A value-based fee appreciates the power of interspace, the knowledge that energy is moving between us whether we're in physical contact or not. I find a lot of healing takes place between sessions, from the unfolding of a healing process that is supported by the container of a relationship that both parties continue to nurture with their respective resources.

Those of you not in private practice, or with insurance restrictions on your relationship, may not be able to engage in this value-setting process, but you can find ways where each of you can be clear about what you value. For example, with Lucy, I became a lot more clear, like a selectively permeable membrane, about when I was available and when I wasn't, and what I asked of her in the healing relationship. She paid the fee set by the retreat center, but the value of our work together was reflected in how I decided whether I'd come in on my day off and the level of participation she brought to each session in addition to cash.

You and your partners can consider the value of your relationship in terms of cancellation policies. Late or missed appointments, for example, offer an opportunity to discuss the value of the work from each of your perspectives. If you don't value the time you set aside for this client, he may never get the chance to really look at how he values both your work and his healing process. Non-compliance with treatment, from a value perspective, can lead to some very healing interchanges. Jesse was a young man who initially came to me for energy work because his mother said he had to either see someone for counseling, or move out of the house. She paid for sessions because Jesse was still in school, so after a couple of late arrivals, we talked about his commitment to the work. Our discussion really helped him come to the realization that he was now coming for himself, not Mom. We worked out a deal that if he arrived late he had to spend a certain amount of time weeding my garden after the session (my office was in my farm home, at the time). Well, he got to like the garden work so much, that he proposed he pay me in labor instead of having his Mom pay. Of course, then we had to talk about equal value, etc., which took him to another level of valuing his own healing process. The therapeutic benefit of the garden work soon took on its own value!

These considerations of value and creative approaches to achieve value for both parties align themselves with the way cell membrane receptors shift and grow. Receptors respond to changes in their environment to achieve sufficient distribution of resources among cells and organs. Your considerations of sufficiency and value can do the same for your healing relationships. There are more ways to mimic cells as you ensure sufficiency and balance of resources.

Commit yourself to make the most of the resources that are available for healing.

Lynne Twist says, "What you appreciate, appreciates," and I've found this to be true in healing relationships. If you only have so much time or your client only has so much money, how can you collaborate to make the most of what you do have? By doing so, the total resource available to you expands. With only three sessions authorized by insurance, maybe you can spread them out with lots of homework or research for your partner to do in between sessions, thereby expanding what's available to her. Can you do work exchange with a colleague that allows each of you time off for family or continuing education? Instead of viewing a referral to someone else (who may be better suited to meet the client's needs) as a loss in your income, you could create a network of referral sources whereby each of you knows and appreciates the different skills you all provide. Within this network of collaborators, everyone prospers by making the most of the available resources, just like the cells in your body do. As a hospital social worker, I often engaged the insurance case manager in a creative and collaborative effort to make the most of the patient's insurance benefits, often exchanging one benefit for another that best suited the need.

Be flexible and creative.

When we don't allow ourselves to be locked into the "there's not enough" myth, and appreciate the resources that are available through creative collaboration, what we value expands to benefit the whole system of which we're a part. I once worked with Jennifer, who was a master organic gardener, and a great cook. She was involved in "Community Supported Agriculture" (CSA) in which people subscribe to receiving a bag of organically grown vegetables each week throughout the growing season. Several farmers contributed to each bag and got a share of the profit. Jennifer didn't have a lot of cash, but her other resources carried great value for me. She asked me if I would be willing to take a fresh-baked loaf of bread or vegetable casserole in lieu of part of the fee I was charging at the time. I gardened and cooked myself, so I knew how much went into growing and baking. I also knew I couldn't pay my office rent with bread or casseroles, so we worked out something that seemed fair to both of us. You may begin to see how the value of what we brought to our work together also enhanced the flow of energy throughout our community. The cash she gave me came from what my neighbors gave her for growing food for them. The health benefit she received from the energy work enabled her to maintain her participation in the CSA. My family enjoyed wholesome food, and 10 years later my son can still buy Jennifer's produce at the local farm stand.

Contain the distribution of resources and responsibility for healing within the primary relationship as much as possible.

Even if your healing partner's hand is far away from the dollar that finds its way into your pocket, i.e. you're paid by an insurance company, an agency, or as in Jesse's case, a parent, you can find ways to keep the flow and responsibility for healing within the relationship you have with your partner. Jesse's work in the garden helped contain the resource flow within our relationship and reflected his responsibility for his own healing. Within an agency or clinic, you can take a minute to mentally link with the fact that in order to be in your treatment space, your partner had to give something of value to be there: time and talent in a job that offers health insurance, walking the labyrinth of application for welfare, or paid taxes to help fund the agency. He may have had to make time, and value his own healing, in order to even recognize the need for treatment. In this way, you are bringing your attention to the value of whatever resource was expended to enter the healing space you create together. Take stock of whatever it is each of you is bringing to the space.

Regardless of who's paying for and authorizing treatment, each of you carries 100% responsibility for what you bring personally to the healing relationship and what begins to flow in interspace. You could acknowledge that even though someone else may influence the amount of time and money available for treatment, the responsibility for what happens in the time you have rests within the potency of your relationship. Just that awareness alone can make a difference in how empowered you each feel in the work. Even if your partner isn't directly paying you, you can invite his full participation in making choices about his care and follow-up treatment.

When you give what you have in time, talent and heart without doing more than is good for you, you contribute to a balanced distribution of resources and responsibility for the healing process.

This idea is especially important with involuntary clients. If someone is ordered to be in treatment by a judge or a parent, the person's physical presence may initially be the only resource he brings into the room. Genuinely appreciate that, and watch how it appreciates.

~~~~~

All of the above strategies work together to bring awareness to the value of the resources that you and your healing partners bring to your relationships. To whatever extent you use your creativity and flexibility to collaborate with your partner around money and resource issues, the awareness that grows from that will enhance the healing and help to dispel the myths our receptors carry around scarcity. Some of our creative strategies can make us vulnerable to ethical misconduct, however, so let's consider that next.

Cautionary Notes

Gifts from Clients

Gifts from clients are frowned upon by most professional organizations, but sometimes they serve to balance resources and facilitate healing. Tips, for example, are commonly given as part of the compensation in health spas, because the clients know the practitioner only gets a percentage of the total fee paid for the service. It's the client's way of balancing the resources between the one actually providing the care and the one providing the space, the bones, if you will, of the healing relationship. A tip can also be a genuine expression of gratitude for the value received from the practitioner. Sometimes, however, the tip can carry the energy of control or express the low self-esteem of the client who feels unworthy of such beautiful work. The receptors we carry can alert us to these and other situations in which the tip sends a message other than a clear exchange of value. Rather than set a boundary against tipping, the cell membrane principles invite us to work with the consciousness awakened by our receptors to meet the energy of the tip with healing intent.

A client once brought me a pot of tulips in gratitude for "saving her life." By accepting the gift and her gratitude, I used the symbolism of the tulip—a bulb that lies dormant until the warmth and light of spring allows it to bloom—to reflect her healing process. I helped her contain the power and responsibility for her own healing (the potential in the bulb), while also acknowledging the value of the healing relationship as the container, the warm spring earth in which the healing happened. If I had refused the gift, I would have been refusing the joy she felt that morning in celebration of her "new life." The cell membrane principles helped me discern, based on the receptors I noticed in her and in myself, the intent of the gift and my response to it. The monetary value of the gift that's offered is less important than its intent. It's a fine line, to be sure, but nature wants us to refine and hone our receptors, and that happens at the fine line—at the edges where our membranes meet for healing.

Bartering

When the exchange of resources represents something other than a mutually agreed upon value for a particular service, like the homemade bread I got from Jennifer, you can easily slip into a dual relationship. For example, your client may not be able to pay you in cash, but is willing to do your bookkeeping, give you a massage or baby-sit for your children. In these instances, you may be opening up more receptors to the relationship than you can consciously be present with at any given time. The next chapter is devoted to the subject of dual relationships, their pitfalls and potentials. For now, however, just keep in mind when you're collaborating and being creative with a healing partner, that it's important to contain the resource exchange to what you each value for the service provided in a way that feels balanced for both of you. If I didn't value Jennifer's cooking as much as cash, or accepted it out of a feeling of charity, the resource exchange would carry that current. If, on the other hand, Jennifer wore herself out growing and cooking food for me, the food would carry a currency of fatigue and not serve her healing. If Jesse did a sloppy job in my garden, it would reflect the value he attributed both to the relationship and his participation in it.

Money and Integral Healing

In the last chapter on power, we looked at the concentric, interactive spheres of power that influence the course of healing for someone with a digestive problem. In an integral health system, healing partners are aware of the embedded realms of influence on the healing outcome. As we've just seen in this chapter, the availability of resources to support a healing partnership depends on the functioning of the other systems in which the healing relationship is imbedded. As the above strategies point out, we can work within the relationship, or anywhere within the sphere of influence, to facilitate the flow of resources through the relationship. Figure 7 depicts these relationship realms of influence with regard to the money available in a healing relationship.

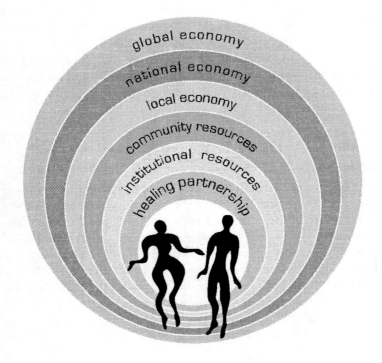

Figure 7. Embedded realms of influence on resources available to a healing relationship

From inner to outer realms:

- individuals in a healing partnership
- institutional resources (hospital, clinic, spa, private practice)
- community resources (insurance companies, employers, welfare agencies)
- local economy
- national economy
- global economy.

Summing up Money

Because money is one of the currencies of exchange among human "cells," it behooves us to notice the issues it raises in our healing relationships. If you think thoughts about money aren't there, or out of the scope of the work you're doing, you may find yourself tripping over it on the way to "higher" aspirations. In so doing, you will miss the opportunity money offers, like water, to keep things clean in a healing relationship. Whether you're clarifying the value of the work you're doing, collaborating with clients and colleagues to increase the resources available to those you serve, or helping clients acknowledge the value of their well-being, money can be a conduit for healing. With an eye to how your practice fosters the balanced flow of resources among partners who collaborate and share responsibility for the healing that happens, money can take its rightful place next to your licenses, certificates and heart as a resource in the healing process.

Chapter 13

THE PROMISE AND PITFALLS OF DUAL RELATIONSHIPS

When I first studied cell physiology over 40 years ago, the job description of each kind of cell was pretty rigid. Blood, kidney, lung and all the other tissue cells had particular jobs to do, armed, we thought, with only those receptors that related to the work of blood, kidney, lung, etc. Then in the 1990s, Candace Pert shook up the cellular biology world with her research that showed far more multi-task job descriptions for the cells in our body. Cells had primary jobs all right but when emotions were involved, cells did more than one thing with one another. I learned about stomach cells having receptors for emotional messages that I thought were only in the brain at about the same time my family therapist moved next door to my best friend. Shortly before that, I found myself working on the same rehabilitation team with a physician who was not only the father of one of my son's good friends, but he also treated both my husband and me for our back problems.

Since then, I've often navigated the rough waters of what professionals call a "dual relationship"—engaging in more than one relationship with a healing partner. We've all been guided by our codes of ethics to avoid dual relationships. The reason for this is to protect both healing partners from the minefield these relationships often represent. Yet, many of us often find ourselves unavoidably thrown into dual relationships, often accompanied by a lot of anxi-

ety. At the same time, I, and maybe you, have found that dual relationships are more than unavoidable—they offer the potential for
rich and rewarding differentiated relationships. Like Bruce Lipton
said, differentiation is nature's way of distributing the workload
among members of a community. If cells are capable of performing
more than one job at a time, and the cell membrane manages all
those jobs, could what we know about how the cell membrane works
help us be in those relationships in a way that supports healing and
doesn't do harm?

I was trying to answer that question for this book, and having a hard time doing it, when I awakened from a dream one morning, which left me with a deep sense of shame. Disturbed and puz-
zled, I explored the dream by taking the feelings into my body,
where I was surprised to find family patterns I thought I'd long ago
arisen above. Risen above in my mind, yes, but here in my body
each of these patterns still lived in my receptors and unconsciously
worked their way into important relationships.

The shame came from deep in my bones. I found myself
putting my thumb in my mouth, seeking the comfort I had known as
a child. I called two friends, Inika and Yavelow, who are also colleagues and, yes, occasionally my therapists. I asked if they would
work with me in the way we work as a team with others. I was grateful when they agreed to help at that early hour—friends do that. But
as I drove to the pool, I began to feel ashamed for asking them for
help—afraid to have them see me like this. It was hard to face them
in such a vulnerable state. Yet it wasn't the first time they'd seen me
unglued, nor me them, and I knew their skills enough to understand
that there were no two people I trusted more or who were better able
to help me transform this shame.

When we met at the pool, I could barely look them in the
eye. There was that thumb that involuntarily kept going in my 63-
year-old mouth as I sobbed before them in shame. They held me in
the water in the space between their hearts—a place where the
shame felt safe. They attentively followed as my body unwound and
released the old patterns, guiding the energy with their skillful touch.

I felt safe enough to reveal the ugliness inside and receive the light of their love. In less than 40 minutes, I was able to feel compassion for those family members with whom I shared a set of receptors now changed by my compassionate and skilled friends.

The amazing complexity and magic of that session was just what I needed to get myself unstuck in my writing too. It took me to a deeper understanding of both the potential and the pitfalls of dual relationships. I watched the principles of the cell membrane reveal themselves as my friends helped me contain my experience, and not react emotionally to what I was doing and saying. They held their Center and helped me find mine. They opened the differentiated receptors from all we'd been through with each other over the years to the healing interspace we created that morning. Inika and Yavelow were able to make conscious choices about which receptors they'd activate and which messages they would send into interspace. As I reflect on the development of the relationships I enjoy with these two special people, I see how we have navigated our multiple relationships in order to avoid the pitfalls (or learn from them when we fell), and mine their potential. We have woven our relationship into a healing tapestry. The cell membrane model, in its flexibility, differentiation potential and oneness is up to the task in guiding us through these complex relationships.

Pitfalls of Dual Relationships

When I first met Yavelow, he was an assistant instructor in my first Watsu (aquatic bodywork) class, and also gave me a professional session as part of the practicum portion of the training. Inika, an instructor in Healing Dance (a related aquatic modality), demonstrated her work later in my training. So our relationships began as professional ones, with them as my teachers. As I relate the development of our relationships over the years, I'll begin with how we faced the inevitable pitfalls of engaging in both professional and personal relationships with our healing partners.

Exploitation of client and therapist vulnerability

Codes of ethics guide us away from exploiting the therapeutic relationship for personal or monetary gain, or taking advantage of the client's vulnerability to satisfy our own needs. Those in physical, emotional or spiritual pain can lose their usual sense of discernment, their ability to make wise choices, so if a therapist uses the relationship to advance a personal agenda (conscious or unconscious) for connection, love or financial gain, safety and trust are severely violated. Conversely, if therapists become too dependent on healing partners for their personal or financial needs, they risk hurting themselves as well. Dual relationships make both partners more vulnerable to harm, but especially the one who comes for help.

I was quite vulnerable when I received that aquatic bodywork session from Yavelow during my training. Everything seemed to be changing in my life just then, leaving my emotions quite frayed and longing for comfort. I was almost startled by how safe I felt being held by a man I'd just met, safe enough for those frayed emotions to surface and be taken by the water. It was Yavelow's presence and his ability to help me first contain, then release, those feelings, that gave me a deep appreciation of the power of this work to help someone heal from loss and longing. A part of me was also observing how the intimacy of the work could so easily slip into exploitation of a partner's vulnerability. Yet there he was, so centered in an interspace uncontaminated by his own longings or loss, that I felt both safe and even cherished in a transpersonal way.

The next morning, after a night of dreams in which I felt myself floating in bliss, I looked for Yavelow as we gathered for class. I told him how grateful I was and how much better I felt. I really praised his work and went on and on about the potential for Watsu to heal issues around intimacy, nurture and trust. Again, it would have been so easy for him to take the credit for how good I felt, or suggest we meet later for a private session, but he didn't. He just smiled with that "all in a day's work" look of his.

Sometimes it's the therapist who is vulnerable. What if Yavelow had needed to know that a woman felt safe and cherished

151

in his arms, or wanted to feel her close to him? He could be vulnerable to a seduction that could backfire if he got dropped after she got her needs met. That didn't happen with us, however, and a foundation of trust was formed between us for the friendship that followed months later when we were both living in the same community.

Transference and counter transference

Yavelow avoided falling into the pitfall of transference and counter transference problems that can arise in dual relationships. He didn't accept any attribution that I tossed his way about the power of his work. While, of course, he had cultivated such a quality, he wasn't about to make himself vulnerable to a countertransference dynamic.

Issues around sexuality or intimacy aren't the only ones that can lead to a transference/countertransference pitfall. The client who begins to regard us as the ideal parent or healer can be devastated to find out in a personal relationship that we're actually human and full of faults. Or we could lock on to their ideal picture of us, masking our own inadequacy receptors, and keep playing that role to our mutual detriment. Serious dependency problems arise in these situations that block the healing process. Here's how Inika and I managed the transference/countertransference pitfall.

Inika's work was beautiful, her voice soft, her descriptions clear and her movement exquisite as she demonstrated her work in our class. I was so inspired that I knew I would take every class she offered. Not only did she seem like the ideal teacher, but almost like a goddess. When we ended up living in the same small community, our initial friendship was limited by my "goddess worship." Of course, since Inika didn't think of herself as a goddess, and we discovered many common interests in addition to bodywork, our budding friendship replaced my idealized projections with a more realistic appreciation of her qualities.

Unclear expectations and intentions, performance anxiety

Months later, I had to be evaluated by Inika in order to be allowed to offer Watsu therapy at the retreat center where we lived and worked. This was one of her jobs, friendship or not. The dual role made it much more difficult for me. I really wanted to get on staff doing the work I loved. And because I admired her work so much and liked her as a friend, I felt even more pressure to perform well. In spite of all that inner expectation and tension, I gave her what I thought was a pretty good session. All the other people I'd practiced on thought I was great! Well, Inika wasn't so sure I was ready yet. This was a possible pitfall for her, too. She wanted to pass her friend, but she had to close her friendship receptors and open only those that took in my professional ability for review. She used both her friendship and professional skills (differentiation) to tell me, in a way that I heard clearly, exactly what it was I needed to work on to pass muster. I was disappointed and hurt, yes, but my respect for her grew. I knew I could trust her to tell me the truth, and she trusted me to take it. I also trusted that she would not tell others in our community about the evaluation, honoring my container.

A few months later, I took my first class from Inika and again she was able to be very clear in her evaluation, to guide me as any good teacher would, unmoved by what she knew I wanted to hear. Soon thereafter, I did gain admission to the aquatic staff. With all these relationship challenges, our ability to be conscious of which receptors were active in each of us and make choices about which ones we would work with made these shifts in roles possible and healthy.

When Inika was going through a difficult time and asked me for a therapeutic session, I faced yet another possible pitfall in this multiple relationships. Doubts about my ability to help her surfaced in ways they rarely do in sessions with clients who aren't my friends, teachers or evaluators. Because she was in pain, my personal self wanted so badly to make it go away. It's the same with Yavelow when I give him a therapy session; I so want him to feel better. Sometimes I want to impress them with some new approach I've developed. All of these feelings are natural in multiple relationships, and if not contained, can really muddy the healing waters.

Yet it usually only takes about 10 minutes into a session with these friends for all the receptors related to performance and expectations to speak up, let me know they're there, and ask for a little attention from me. Once they're soothed, and I come to Center, the healing work can happen from that place that is beyond the concerns of the ego. Such a process, rather than detracting from the healing process, actually serves the differentiation process. More consciousness is brought to the receptors and the support helps them differentiate and be less reactive the next time. If it isn't possible to differentiate among competing receptors, and make choices about which ones you'll make available, it may be best not to work on friends.

Trades

Trading sessions is very common in the bodywork community. It starts in the training, where we practice the techniques on each other in class. Other professions use guinea pigs (of various species) or cadavers or real live wounded people to practice their craft. It seems quite natural, however, for bodyworkers to continue trading sessions once we're practicing professionally. I need a massage and know a friend who gives a good one, so I offer to trade sessions. This doesn't happen in quite as clear a way in other health fields; occupational therapists don't fit each other with hand braces, and psychotherapists don't exchange sessions. So, while most of what I say here about trades applies only to bodyworkers, other health care professionals might want to think of the more subtle ways friends and colleagues "treat" each other, and notice how it affects their relationships.

Trades are ridden with pitfalls. What if you're asked for a session from a colleague who offers a trade, and you don't necessarily like her work, or you just prefer to get your therapy from someone else? How about those times when you give someone a great treatment, but then can't coordinate your schedules when it's your turn? Months pass by before you get payment. There are times when

I need cash more than I need bodywork, or need more bodywork than I have the energy to pay back in sessions. You might consider mutually determining a value on the work you're willing to trade, and paying each other the same amount—trading the same dollar back and forth. That acknowledges the value of resources flowing between you and keeps the relationship more clearly in balance.

Healing Potential of Dual Relationships

If dual relationships present us with all kinds of opportunity for getting ourselves stuck in emotional taffy with our healing partners, often resulting in hurt to both, why don't we just avoid them altogether, like the codes of ethics suggest? Cell membranes show us that it's possible to create complex relationship systems that work for the benefit of the whole. If we follow nature's model, we can avoid the pitfalls and realize the healing potential of dual relationships, which basically reflect nature's tendency toward differentiation and health through diversity. We're interconnected beings, after all, and rather than avoid that reality, we best learn how to function in multiple relationships in ways that honor our nature.

Try as we might to keep our personal and professional lives separate, nature has a way of sending tendrils of life through the stones in the walls we construct between our different worlds. That was embarrassingly clear when I was hospitalized years ago. I needed to be catheterized by the doctor I had stood beside as we cheered our sons on in swim team! When we later became colleagues on the same rehabilitation team, I had to realize that I couldn't avoid dual relationships. Each of the dual relationships that followed challenged my ability to be conscious of which receptors were operating in which aspect of the relationship, in order to live these relationships according to the ecological principles I was trying to embody. The process helped me differentiate my own criteria for when and how to engage in more than one relationship with someone with whom I'm also in a professional relationship. People I knew socially who became patients in the hospital where I worked, hospital patients who decided to take a workshop I offered, teachers who became friends, all took me to those co-creative edges that challenged my ability to manage more than one relationship with someone.

Did I make mistakes? Boy, did I! I hurt (and was hurt by) others when I wasn't fully aware of what was happening in me and the other person. It would have been easier, and a few times much less hurtful, to have avoided dual or multiple-relationships with clients or teachers altogether. However, not as much healing would have happened either. By dancing on the edges that these kinds of relationships drag us into, I have learned something that informs me about the unfathomable depths we're capable of when we consciously dance with others in healing. The hard work of dual relationships exercises our receptors, renders and reshapes them. They forge us into healthier therapists with a greater capacity to meet our clients where they are, with a highly differentiated set of receptors at their service.

When I work with Yavelow in a session, for example, the compassion and trust borne of all the ways we relate to each other becomes available to his healing, and the healing seems to go deeper. The fact that he's witnessed my vulnerability helps him to be vulnerable. My personal relationship with Inika is enriched by our receptor honing experiences together as teacher, student and therapist. With each of these friends, we also have to face the limitations in what we can do therapeutically together—that's part of differentiation also. We are not each other's primary therapists; friendship is the primary relationship that has professional aspects to it—like the stomach cells that primarily serve digestion, but also respond to emotional signals. We function in separate roles that come together when needed to get another job done.

Inika, Yavelow and I were joined by my life partner, Jim, a couple of years ago in circumstances that took our collective relationship to new levels. We'd all had training and experience in various forms of "multi-hand" therapy, in which several people work at the same time with the one receiving treatment. Jim had to differentiate a bit to bring his energy healing and craniosacral skills into the water, and all four of us had to shift from doing our own thing to working as a team. In our multi-handed team, each of us brought our separate skills in at least 10 different modalities to those sessions, but something amazing happened when we began to come together.

The experiences deeply touched us, both in what we experienced as a team and especially what we observed in those we worked on. We'd practiced first on each other, working three-on-one, and although we found the sessions to be quite extraordinary, we weren't sure how it would be for those who weren't close friends. As we invited various clients we knew from our individual practices to try a multi-hand session, we observed responses we hadn't seen when we worked with them alone. Places of pain and emotional trauma released much more easily. More than just ease was involved, however as clients reported that, within minutes, they experienced themselves as a part of something larger than their individual self. The pain and trauma didn't seem as personal as when we worked alone—they just met each restriction in turn and watched it flow away. The kind of support they experienced felt less personal as well—like being held by one vast organism, not four separate therapists. We all experienced the principle of Oneness in action.

Just about that time, a client told me about a book she was reading, *Emergence* by Steven Johnson, that described the life cycle of slime mold, a single-celled organism that lives on the forest floor. For a good part of its life cycle, the slime mold functions as an individual cell doing its own thing in the forest. All at once, in response to a signal arising within and among the individual slime mold cells, they form a web along the forest floor that creeps along as one slimy organism decomposing and transforming fallen leaves into nurturing soil. "That's what we're doing," I told my partners. "We're functioning like slime mold!" My friends didn't think the "Slime Mold Team" would sell on our brochures, but we sure felt a resonance with the process. Reading further into *Emergence*, I learned that scientists looked hard for something that controlled this process in slime molds and other living systems, only to conclude, when they found no "master," that they were "self-organizing" systems. No, our team doesn't need for one of us to be boss, because over the years we've brought our consciousness to the web of love that powers our work together. When we link with that web, something bigger than our individual selves guides the work. We bring the one we hold into that web, and healing unfolds.

When you choose to consciously enter nature's web as you do your work with others, you will inevitably be drawn into differentiated relationships, relationships that ask you to do more than one thing at a time, and hold your awareness of individuality and Oneness at the same time. The more we practice according to ecological principles, the less able we'll be to place a boundary around our relationships, and that's where these same cell membrane principles can help us manage the challenge.

Dual relationships demand more consciousness, more flexibility and more of a willingness to take what's evoked in them into our own development. The pitfalls I pointed out earlier show up in different ways with different partners, and not everyone is ready developmentally, or willing to engage in dual relationships with clients or patients. Selective permeability gives you the choice of when and to what extent you feel you can handle more than one relationship with a partner. It's quite okay to avoid them until you feel you're ready. As you test the waters and explore the possibility of entering into a dual relationship, the following guidelines from the cell membrane perspective may help you navigate the rough waters to reach the potential these relationships can offer.

Navigational Skills

Dual relationships with your healing partners may look like the ones I've discussed so far in this chapter, but they take many forms and levels of relationship. You may find yourself going to the same church with one of your partners and ending up on the same committee. You and a patient may each have a child in the same class at school and need to carpool. A family member may come to you with a problem he might think you could help with or a colleague asks to trade sessions without pay. Someone you've worked with as a client may want to help you set up a healing center where your work can reach more people;

another may offer to organize a class for you to teach in a country where you've always wanted to travel. Over the course of treatment, you and a client may develop a profound connection and one or both of you may want to move into a sexual relationship. These are but a few of the many possibilities in which you will be asked to make a choice that fosters healing and avoids doing harm.

Overall, the bottom line is consciousness. How conscious can you be of what is happening in each of the relationships you're engaged in with someone with whom you do healing work? When you're in a healing relationship, the healing needs of the person you're treating must be first and foremost in your awareness. If for any reason, you can't do this, you can't foster healing for that person. It's really okay, even imperative, to recognize what you can and cannot do and say so. That's honoring your own container and the receptors that are asking for your attention. Of course, we're rarely in all-or-nothing circumstances where everything that effects the treatment is always in our awareness. As I've said so often, it's those little unconscious longings and desires that sometimes need healing sessions to come out of hiding. The following questions can guide your inquiry and raise your awareness about what to look for as you ponder mixing therapeutic and personal or business relationships. These questions apply to sexual relationships as well, but since sex comprises a large percentage of the ethical misconduct complaints around dual relationships, I will go into sexual issues in healing relationships in the next chapter of this book.

How many receptors can you be conscious of at the same time?

I find it hard to have my own agenda with someone at the same time I want to be fully present to their healing process. If I want to please someone, release their pain or think about what recently happened in a business meeting, it can be difficult to focus my attention only on the therapeutic nature of what we're there for, to engage only my therapeutic receptors. When thoughts and feelings of a personal or business nature arise in a healing session, we need to be able to contain them and redirect our attention to the work we're there to do.

The receptors (qualities) you develop with friends, lovers or business acquaintances can be brought to bear in a session, but only if they really assist in the therapy. The acceptance and trust I felt with Inika and Yavelow as friends served my healing, but Yavelow's sharp wit would not have been welcome then—and he knew it. The compassion, clarity, and love that grow in a relationship will serve both the healing and personal relationships, but our longings, jealousy, needs and self-doubt can get in the way. In order for a dual relationship to work for healing, you must be able to make conscious choices about what parts of you will be active in a session. It's selective permeability at its best.

Of equal importance is that the person you're doing healing work with is capable of the same level of consciousness about what receptors are active for them and like you make choices about containment. Some vulnerable healing partners aren't developmentally ready to come to the level of self-awareness that's necessary to make such choices, however, and this is where we have to check-in on the potential for runaway transference and countertransference. Your partner (in friendship, love or business) needs to be able don only his patient/client hat and contain the thoughts that you may owe him some money or that he wants to go to bed with you. If he can't do that, a decision needs to be made about which relationship is primary, and either not engage in the second one or moderate it to account for developmental limitations.

A dear friend wanted to receive the benefits of energy work from me many years ago when there weren't many people in our town doing that work. However it didn't take long for him to realize that, with me, he just couldn't allow himself to get into the deep levels of emotional vulnerability that the work was bringing up. We felt he would be better off seeing another therapist because we knew that both our friendship and his healing needs would best be served by keeping them separate. His friendship receptors couldn't function at the same time as his frightened little boy receptors.

How clearly can you communicate which receptors are available and which are not?

Once you're aware of which receptors you want to be functioning when, it's important to be able to clearly communicate that to your partner. Sometimes that can be as simple as saying, "I'm putting on my therapy hat now and I'd like to ask you to . . ." Or, "I'm not feeling up to the level of work you seem to want today, could we find another time?" If your partner is able receive what you say without reacting in a way that adversely affects his healing process, you know a healthy dual relationship is possible.

When something uncomfortable comes up for either of you in the relationship, it's essential that you be able to talk about it openly and honestly. Talking about what's showing up in your receptors helps keep things clear and contained, and allows for each of you to decide what to allow in which relationship.

How readily and consciously can you shift from one relationship container to another?

You and your partner may find yourselves in an intense discussion or heavy treatment session in which a lot of uncomfortable material arises, and then you both show up for the same committee meeting the next day. Can each of you be fully present to the matter at hand without harkening back to what happened in the healing session? Can you contain and work with uncomfortable feelings that arise at the meeting and keep them free from the treatment session next week?

These shifts can be very subtle, dropping into your therapeutic role when called upon and moving into another when that time comes. I don't mean to imply that we become chameleons, just that we learn to activate only those receptors that we want to be active in the different relationship environments.

161

Can you keep the intention for each of the relationships clear?

This question is related to the last question, but offers an important differentiation task. Cells set out receptors dedicated to a specific purpose, and our intentions have a way of activating just those receptors we want to be available to the therapeutic session. The intention of a friendship or business relationship sets out a different group of receptors. You might want to refer back to Chapter 10 where the importance of setting clear intentions is discussed.

How evenly balanced are you and your partner on socio-economic, emotional, mental and spiritual levels?

When there's a large disparity in balance between you and another person on any level of development, dual relationships present a greater risk to the healing relationship. This is also a differentiation matter. If you badly need something your client has (power, sex, money, status, intelligence, spiritual sensitivity), you will be hard-pressed to be fully present to their needs in a healing relationship. If your client feels needy in any of these areas, and sees you as someone who can provide them, again the receptor imbalance is too great to engage in a healthy dual relationship. The saying, "Birds of a feather flock together," applies here. We have a far better chance of developing healthy, co-creative dual relationships when both or all members of the team are at similar levels of development.

Can you both keep confidentiality?

Confidentiality in professional healing work is just that—confidentiality. It doesn't matter that you know and love friends or relatives of your client; what happens to her in your therapeutic sessions is hers to tell—or not. It also helps her to be able to contain some of her own process rather than rippling it through your relationship circle. When each of you maintains confidentiality, the integrity and potency of your therapeutic container remains sound. Good news is especially tempting to tell a common friend. Or you may want to ask someone else to support your client/friend through a particularly rough time. But even if we have our client/friend's best interest at heart, their successes or struggles on the healing path are not ours to share, regardless of intention. In a healthy relationship, we're able to talk openly about what to share outside the relationship.

An exception to keeping confidence is, as always, if your partner poses a risk to himself or others. Even here though, it's important that you be able to tell your partner that you plan to alert others to his need, what you plan to do, etc. This is true in any healing relationship, but the issue could evoke more of your own anxiety if your partner is also a friend, lover or business partner.

Are you willing to seek supervision?

Supervision from a trusted colleague or teacher is extremely helpful when you're not sure how you'd answer some of these questions, or find yourself mired in a relationship dilemma. Supervision offers the kind of reflection needed to let you know exactly what issues this relationship is bringing forward for each of you and how to proceed with awareness and healing intent.

Do you recognize the signals that let you know when the therapeutic relationship is being compromised by personal or business matters?

Knowing the signs of trouble often lets you address a problem before it gets messy. It's yet another way of watching your receptors, knowing which ones are being triggered at what times in dual relationships. Here are some of the signs:

- You begin to look forward to a therapy session as though it were a special date, i.e. your personal longing receptors are active and you are using the therapeutic relationship to meet a personal need.

- You find yourself watching how your friend behaves, eats, or relates through the eyes of a therapist rather than a friend.

163

- Issues that come up in the therapeutic relationship permeate your judgment of your friend or business partner in other settings, and compromise the second relationship.

- You or your partner begin to ignore time limits for treatments.

- Either of you expects special treatment because of the business or personal relationship.

- You fail to be clear about monetary arrangements between you

- You find yourself getting sloppy about other parameters of your therapeutic work together.

- You begin to lose clarity about when you're doing therapy and when you're not.

- Either of you becomes hesitant to complain when something doesn't feel right in either of the relationships.

There are more signals, I'm sure, but I think you can begin to get the idea that dual relationships ask more of us in awareness, communication and honesty than the more casual relationships that don't include a therapeutic dimension, or therapeutic relationships that don't include any other dimension.

~~~~

A couple of years after Inika and Yavelow helped me transform those family wounds, Inika asked our team of three for a birthday session. In what Carl Jung would definitely call a synchronicity, I happened to be in the middle of rewriting this particular chapter, and was exactly poised to review the section on the potential in dual relationships. There were times during that poignant session, where I stood back a little from the group and just beheld my two beloved friends supporting the third through her healing. I reflected on the fact that humans throughout time have held each other in healing, the same people they hunted or gardened with, or who taught their children essential living skills. When we can integrate the process of healing into the life of a community, we act according to our nature—to be with each other in joy and sorrow, in pain and play. Gratitude and love welled up inside me as I re-joined our team— grateful that we've created this precious tapestry of relationships.

I recognize, however, that precious tapestries need more care than simple fabrics. They take more training and practice to create. The same is true for the integrated relationships that can evolve from dual and multiple relationships with those we engage in healing. The threads of friendship, business and healing can weave themselves together when the intent to create such a tapestry exists alongside the consciousness and dedication to sit at the loom long enough. When threads of sexual energy seek to weave their way into a therapeutic relationship, even more consciousness and care is needed to preserve and honor the healing process. Let's move on to the discussion of how sexuality can bring us to the edge of power to harm and heal in our relationships.

Chapter 14

SEXUALITY: CO-CREATIVITY IN THE HEALING RELATIONSHIP

Sex is the spark of creativity in nature. Sexual energy flows through all dimensions of human consciousness, lending creative potency to all it touches. Sex draws us, consumes us, frightens us, and takes us into communion with the Divine. In your healing partners, you'll find sexual energy attached to issues of survival, love, fear, creativity, joy, control, intimacy and touch, as well as other issues that connect so strongly to health and healing. Because of its power to both harm and heal, we need to learn to work skillfully with sexual energy in our healing relationships, and work with sex in ways that tap its co-creative rather than its harmful potential.

The cell membrane principles we've become familiar with, as we explored their application with issues of safety, money, power and dual relationships, require further scrutiny when it comes to sex. Just as cells had to do when sex evolved on the planet, we need to refine the cell membrane principles even more when sex shows up in our treatment spaces. Sex evolved in nature essentially as a means to creatively solve a problem generated by life itself as it reshaped the Earth's lifeless crust and changed its atmosphere. *As we encounter sexual issues with our healing partners, sex can signal an opportunity to be creative in solving whatever healing challenge it presents.* When working with nature's most creative gift, we're called upon to be even more conscious of which receptors are being activated by the relationship and respond in ways that foster healing. Our response to sexual energy carries a creative impulse into interspace, which affects all life. Let's revisit each of the cell membrane principles with an eye toward how they apply when it comes to sex.

Containment

Cells need to be intact, with all their inherited and learned qualities defined, before they can recombine those qualities with another to co-create something new. You serve your healing partners best when you know yourself and become conscious of what you're bringing into the co-creative process. Likewise, when you help your partners become more familiar with their own container (their body, heart and soul) the chances for a co-creative partnership improve. It doesn't help a healing relationship when partners are unable to contain their sexual longings and desires; when the partners can't contain them, they prevent the creative potency of those feelings from serving the healing process.

As we apply the containment principle to sexuality in healing partnerships, things get a little complicated. In nature, when individual cells get sexual, they physically interpenetrate one another in order to share and recombine genetic material (inherited information) to create something new. Humans, however, have other ways of sharing and recombining information and energy, only one of which, sexual intercourse, involves physical interpenetration. Humans can be co-creative through the exchange of verbal information, for example. Words shared can reorganize themselves into a new idea that neither partner could have come up with alone, making it a co-creative process. The same is true of emotions, sound, color and other forms of energetic expression that can move right through the personal space of your partner, whether you're conscious of it or not. Again, we come to the importance of intention. When you give expression to only those actions, thoughts and feelings that serve your partner's healing, and you contain those that express either partner's personal longings or desires, you honor both the selective permeability and the containment principles.

167

Barbara Marx Hubbard clarified this idea of co-creative sexuality in a one-minute video she offered to the Institute for Noetic Sciences:

> *"One of my favorite words and experiences is supra-sex—not super sex—supra-sex. I think something funda-mental is happening, that the desire to join with others to reproduce the species is expanding into the desire to express unique creativity, and when you meet somebody who excites your capacity to create, you get what I call vocational arousal. Nature put joy into procreation—nature is putting joy into co-creation, and I think the way we are actually going to transform the world is not by fear or guilt or power or domination, but by supra-sexual co-creation."*

Containment, along with the other cell-membrane principles, guides us toward the co-creative relationship with our healing partners that Hubbard refers to.

Selective Permeability

Selective permeability gets quite a workout when it comes to sex. Living things have learned over billions of years to be highly selective about which cells to snuggle up to when old knowledge needs to be reshaped into something new on the planet. Likewise, when dealing with sexual issues between healing partners, the more conscious we are of which receptors have been activated in both partners by the session, the more likely it will be that we will choose a healing versus hurtful or wounding message to send into interspace.

Human consciousness, with all its personal, interpersonal and transpersonal dimensions, affords us many choices in how we respond to sexual energy in relationships. For example, let's say you find yourself looking forward to your next appointment with someone. You really like him and notice that you think of him a lot between sessions. He's handsome, warm and, oh, so responsive to you. The containment and selective permeability principles guide you into your own receptor field where you'll find all kinds receptors buzzing at the thought of this man. He fits your attractiveness template just fine! He sets your heart receptors to a loving tune and your *urge-to-merge* receptors sing out for action. So now you know it—that's great. Now comes the decision about what you want to *do* with those feelings to serve his healing intention. One choice is to jam your feelings behind a boundary. That may work for a while, but the cell membrane model has already shown us that suppressed feelings have a way of finding their way right on through our mental concept of a boundary. Once in interspace they can tickle your partner's receptors, the very ones that may have already been acting as magnets for your longings, unbeknownst to either of you. The boundary you thought you put there merely added force to the magnetism, and you're feeling the pressure.

Another choice is to set your *urge-to-merge* messages free in interspace, along with all the other feelings. After all, doesn't this feel like a unique and rare situation—one that may never come around again? Codes of ethics to the rescue! Well, maybe. Sometimes that prohibition against personal or sexual relationships with clients just amps up the sexual energy seeking expression—like a hurricane surge against a levy. So what's a responsible therapist to do? What would nature want us to do?

Selective permeability and containment join hands to guide you. If you track, contain and support your own longings, you may discover something about your own sexual process that needs attending to, something that has nothing to do with this partner. You can embrace and even celebrate the sexual aliveness in yourself without attributing what you're feeling to this particular partner. Possibilities abound when you contain and work with what's been activated in the relationship. When you support your partner's containment and choose what messages to send and receive from him, he too can discover more of what's active in him. I'm not pretending that this is an easy process. Nature has worked over three billion years to hone its skills around sexuality. As Earth's youngest species,

169

we've still got a lot to learn. Let's look at how you might choose among all your competing sexual receptors in this situation.

You can start by containing any messages that come from the personal dimension of your consciousness: your longing for release or expression of your sexual tension, your need to feel attractive, powerful, etc. Thank your receptors for letting you know how important this is to you and promise you'll pay attention to them another time. Right now you've got other work to do. By not judging your longings and desires as wrong, unprofessional or inappropriate, you bathe them in compassion. But another dimension of receptors has been activated, too. You can allow those messages that convey transpersonal love for your partner, or the ones that recognize his qualities, to flow into interspace. Your compassion can be there as well. Here, the interpersonal field is filled only with regard and compassion, not personal longing or desire. If you've cultivated the transpersonal receptors that recognize the Oneness in all human experience, you can activate those in order to embrace your experience without judgment. By differentiating the dimensions of consciousness that are active through your attraction, you bring selective permeability to a more mature level of relationship, one that can serve co-creative healing.

Interspace and Oneness

When sexual energy is present, interspace and Oneness become even more prominent principles in your healing relationships. By bringing your awareness to the effect of sexual expression on the larger systems of which you're a part, you can become a more active and conscious partner in personal, professional, community and planetary evolution, which I'll get into later in the chapter. These principles remind us that the creative outcomes of our healing relationships touch more than two people. When we act out of alignment with nature's way around sexuality, we wound others as well as ourselves.

Differentiation

Living things really let their creativity flow once sexuality evolved. All the diversity of life we now appreciate—and, ironically, destroy—bears witness to this creative expression through sexuality. Over millennia, receptors on cell membranes developed increasing sensitivity to discern subtle shifts in their environment, which signaled the right conditions for sex. Some receptors respond to specific sounds or aromas. Temperature and light often have to be just right before nature uses her creative gift to send something new into the next generation. When we, as health practitioners, can embrace sexuality not only as a reproductive process, but a differentiating one, we can engage its power to take our partners and us into new and co-creative outcomes in their healing process.

The differentiation process guides us out of habitual responses and into co-creative ones. You may notice, for example, that you react in a predictable way to sexual issues that present in your healing sessions. That's a good start. You might also notice, for example, that your receptors are tuned to "Hit the Road, Jack!" or maybe "Love Me Tender." By tracking, containing and supporting what you notice about your habitual reaction, you may discover a larger repertoire of tunes as you connect to Center.

Your partner might benefit from some differentiating of his receptors also. Maybe he's been tuned to "Can't Get No Satisfaction" but hasn't yet learned that his receptors are ready for retuning. Or maybe the "Can't Get No Satisfaction" receptor is drowning out the "I'm Just a Lonely Boy" receptor. You can help him differentiate by inquiring more into what his action or words are saying about his receptor field, thereby offering him more choices about how he wants to respond.

The differentiation principle works for us the same way it works for cells that want to solve a problem in a new, co-creative way. Differentiation gives each partner a chance to get to know their receptors better in an interspace free of judgment, which could appreciably change their reactivity around sexuality. You could respond to a difficult situation by simply putting up a boundary and saying something like, "This is a professional relationship and it's inappropriate for you to . . ." and stop the behavior—but the differentiating opportunity would be lost. In a worst case, it could be just the boundary your partner needs to try even harder to engage you in interpersonal sex. If he tries harder and you reinforce your boundary, his seduction receptors become recharged with the habitual tunes along with your resistant ones. Any reactive and judgmental comment (even couched in nice professional language) that communicates, "You're just like all MEN," also re-energizes the old messages in each of you that men are only interested in sex. By clearly looking at which receptors are buzzing in both of you and openly and clearly communicating that, you take a differentiating step.

Most situations that ask for a co-creative response will be more subtle than a direct seductive message, however. What does that touch or smile or comment really mean? When does your partner's charm or even withdrawal or fear signal a sexual wound? Which sexual issues underlie chronic health or emotional problems, and how can you help your partner become aware of their impact to support healing? I've found that when I can view sexual energy as a signal that something is ready to shift and grow in my healing partner or myself, I'm more likely to respond in a healing way. In some people, sexual wounds block access to the life-enhancing energy they need for their healing. So whether sexual energy is signaling a readiness for healing, or its wounds are contributing to symptoms of disease, our ability to track, contain and support our partners and ourselves around sexual issues will impact the quality of our healing relationships.

The following suggestions serve as guidelines toward more response and less reaction in order to avoid doing harm in everyday practice around sexual issues with your clients. They are not intended to help you become a sex therapist, which requires specialized training.

Keys to Working Skillfully with Sexual Issues in Healing Relationships

Examine your personal, family and cultural sexual stories and how those stories show up as activated receptors in your healing relation - ships.

The stories about sex that you and I were told as we grew up vary from family to family, yet also reflect commonly held cultural stories at any given time. Behavior in relationships follows and reinforces story, and stories are stored in our receptor field until experience, knowledge and expanded consciousness foster a shift in the story. The story I grew up with about sexuality goes a little like this:

> Storks bring babies. Sex is something you don't talk about, unless adults joke about it and then it's a dirty joke that gets a lot more laughs than other jokes. We should be ashamed of ourselves if we let anyone see us naked, but it's okay if men look at magazines with pictures of naked women in them. Girls are not to "let a boy take advantage of" them, and boys are supposed to try to get to first and second base with a girl on the way to scoring a home run. These games continue into adulthood when you fall in love, get married, and then it's okay to score all the home runs you want to, as long as you score only with your spouse. Of course women still talk with women about the games they play to both attract and resist their husbands, and men continue to power up their game so they can keep scoring. "Being intimate" was the same as "having sex" which was defined narrowly as sexual intercourse. Sex is approved of between young, married, white, middle-class, and able-bodied heterosexuals—in everyone else, it's dirty—and we're back to the dirty jokes. And, by the way—it's okay to treat the Earth like dirt.

Can't you just imagine the confused receptors I carried into puberty? Fortunately for me, the differentiation principle was also at work, which allowed knowledge and experience to reshape and retune those receptors. I told a different story to my children than the one I was told, and now my heart warms at the sight of my grand-children tenderly touching their mommies' bellies and talking to their new baby brother or sister inside. They're delighted to run naked, and play in the bathtub with one another without anyone telling them they need to be ashamed of their bodies. Yet their young sexual receptors are still bathed in the confusing messages of our culture. They're growing up at a time when conservatives, liberals and religious sects are fighting over control of their bodies and deciding who they can marry and when. Thousands of their peers around the world are sold into sexual slavery, while countless others are being abused in their own homes and neighborhoods. The "bat-tle of the sexes" still rages, and sexual organs and weapons of war still bear similar names. My grandchildren are growing up at a time when sex sells everything from toothpaste to automobiles and 11 million viewers watch the Victoria's Secret annual lingerie show on television. One of the models for that show was quoted as saying, "You get butterflies and sweaty palms, but when you do it, it's amaz-ing and empowering. If you can wear a bra and panty on the runway, you overcome all your other insecurities." So even though these sex-ual stories still tune our receptors in the power and control frequen-cy, many of us are expanding our frequency spectrum to embrace the heart, communication, and spiritual dimensions of sexuality.

As I mentioned earlier, you have an opportunity in your healing relationships to examine how the sexual stories carried by receptors can differentiate and contribute to personal and planetary healing and evolution. Let's look at Lance and Sheila, who didn't know how much their family stories were driving their healing rela-tionship and how the cell membrane model could have fostered heal-ing instead of harm.

Lance and Sheila

Lance, a fairly new bodywork practitioner, grew up with a rather confusing set of messages around sexuality. He admired his father's power and charisma, his attractiveness to women, but also saw how much his father's behavior was hurting his mother. Early in life, he became his mother's confidant and protector, and vowed, when he became a man, to always treat women with respect. Women, therefore, loved and trusted Lance; he was gentle and understanding, just like he was with his mother.

Sheila was very close to her father, so close that Dad would often come to her room alone and fondle her breasts and genitals. He was always gentle and loving and never hurt her physically. In her initial therapeutic massage sessions with Lance, she felt safe and cared for, since he always maintained good boundaries. Sheila even found that by receiving his quality of touch she was able to be open and feel more intimacy with her husband.

One morning, Sheila arrived for a massage fresh from a weekend workshop in which she'd experienced a spiritual awakening. She asked Lance if he would include her breasts in the massage; she so wanted to experience the wholeness of her body. "I trust you," she said, "and know you won't violate any boundaries." He didn't realize how her request had activated those receptors formed by his need to take care of his mother. Lance proceeded with her request, unaware of his *I'll take care of you* messages moving through interspace.

That night, Sheila awakened with a dream memory of being alone with her father. For the first time, she felt ashamed about Daddy. The part of her emerged that knew all along that the sexual fondling didn't feel right, the part that stayed out of her awareness until touched by Lance. The next day she reported Lance's behavior to the massage certification board.

If Lance had known about and followed the five-step process, he would have taken the time in the session to help Sheila contain her spiritual awakening and to ground it in her own being. He didn't realize that in such a state of ecstatic light, it isn't unusual for the light to shine on an old wound, making it more available for healing. He also would have been more likely, by checking what was activated in him, to discover those old *Mom-pleasing* receptors at work. In situations like incest, it's not uncommon for a therapist's caring touch to be experienced by a client's wounded receptors like the touch of their parent, who may also have been telling himself he was just loving and caring for his daughter. Add to that Lance's need to help women feel good about themselves and you have a recipe for professional disaster. The five-step process would have further guided Lance into his Center where he might have discovered a way to be present with Sheila's process without inadvertently reactivating her childhood wounds.

Later in this chapter, we'll explore working more skillfully with those who have experienced sexual trauma, but here I just want to emphasize the importance of ongoing scrutiny of our own receptors around sexuality. If we follow the five-Step process, those situations which could spell trouble in our healing relationships will instead inform us which family or cultural stories, stored in our receptor field, are ready for re-tuning and healing.

Practice Containment—over and over and over again.

The next step, of course, once you know which receptors or messages are active for you or your partner, is to contain the message so that it comes more fully into consciousness. This can be quite a challenge, especially when the receptors or messages are charged with nature's creative juice! I've found that when I practice containment outside of therapeutic situations, I'm better able to contain my process in healing sessions. For example, I might notice my reactivity to a scene in a movie, a particular piece of music that evokes a memory, or a passage in a book. Whether the trigger to my receptor is pleasant, like a beautiful love scene or natural landscape, or whether it's something frightening or painful like a lost love or news of a rape, I practice sitting for a moment with the feeling evoked and hold it in my personal space. You can notice which of your sexual buttons get pushed by daily events and then practice containing your reaction. Which of your personal, family or cultural stories is stored in those reactive receptors? What can you do to support yourself and bring compassion to what's been activated?

If the cell membrane model had been part of Lance's bodywork training, he might have been more likely to examine and practice tracking his responses as women came to him for help. What stories did he tell himself about why he was seeing so many women in his practice who so easily surrendered to his touch? What were his fears if he wasn't able to do what they needed? How much did he need to be needed by them? How much did he long to know how much he pleased them?

It's a little harder to practice helping our partners with containment if we're not actually in a session. You can start with the easier issues that ask for containment. For example, if your partner praises you for how good she feels, you could ask her to tell you more about how she's feeling, expand on it a bit. Or it can be as simple as holding in interspace whatever your partner is saying or doing, without any need to do or say anything at all. The more you practice with less intense issues, the easier it is to help your partner contain more highly charged experiences.

Differentiate all the dimensions of human sexual consciousness and practice moving between them in your responses to your heal-ing partners.

I mentioned earlier how humans are capable of many dimensions of sexual, co-creative consciousness other than just the physical or reproductive ones. When it comes to sex, it's often helpful to invite our partners to expand their understanding or experience of what's happening in their healing process. Let's look at a couple of examples:

Ed

I met Ed, early in my hospital social work career, while he was recovering from having his prostate gland removed because of cancer. Slumped in his bed, he didn't seem to be in pain and he easily engaged in planning his home health care. Yet something unsaid was hanging in interspace. "I wonder," I said, "if any of your doctors have talked with you about what you could expect with sexual function following the surgery." He paused, then mumbled, "it's over . . . I'm not a man anymore." Slowly and tenderly we entered his story, the culture's story of what it meant to be a man. He was middle-aged, of my father's time and culture, so I knew it wouldn't be easy for him to talk about sex. "Oh, my wife understands," he said, "it's not that big a deal to her, but . . ."

Over the next several days I held that "but . . ." in interspace and very carefully invited him to complete the sentence, to give us both a more clear sense of which receptors were active and which ones were waiting in the wings to get a differentiation boost. Clearly, his survival from cancer (can't be sexual unless you survive) and his concept of manhood were close together in the sexual spectrum. His story evolved, and more receptors opened, as we explored ways he might stay in touch with his wife and give expression to their needs for touch and intimacy. We also looked at those other activities in life such as strength and protection that need a man. By stepping into communication around sexuality as being more than just the ability to have an erection, Ed gained some understanding and insight into sexual options still available to him. I invited him into the dimension of his heart when I held the space for him to grieve his loss, and he was also able to move into that part of himself that felt fear, both for his

178

survival and sexual function. We brought his wife into our discussions and we all talked with the urologist about options available to him. When he went home, he left with a changed sense of himself as a man. The prostate surgery, which profoundly affected the physical dimension of Ed's sexuality, also opened the door to new creative opportunities for intimacy and touch in his sexual relationship with his wife.

When your healing partners are only seeing one or two dimensions of their sexuality, you can be most helpful by gently inviting them into other dimensions. By doing so, they can disperse a lot of the anxiety or reactivity created by a more limited sexual consciousness. Of course, you can't invite someone to move into areas of awareness around sexuality unless you have learned to dance in those areas yourself. Likewise, your partner may invite you to enter zones you didn't know were active—which is what happened with Roger.

Roger

Roger, a massage therapist, came to me in consultation about what had been happening in his sessions with gay men. Roger is heterosexual, but noticed he'd been attracting a number of homosexual men to his practice. He'd always felt comfortable working with gay men, but suddenly he found himself wanting to distance himself from what felt like sexual energy coming from them. Subtle yet clear boundary setting only increased the sexually suggestive behavior of his clients, along with Roger's discomfort about being the object of their sexual desires. He knew he could terminate these sessions, but was curious enough about what was happening in his own process with these sessions to seek consultation.

In our consultation session, I invited Roger to recall one of these situations with gay men and take the feeling into his body. He was surprised to be called to his heart, rather than lower down in his belly. As we explored further, he entered the childhood memory of lying close to his father in bed on nights when he was frightened by something. As a small boy, he felt safe and warm nestled close to his beloved father. In our session, he began to cry, then sob in grief over his father's death and the awareness that that kind of heart connection was missing in his life right now. Soon, the grief softened and yielded to feeling like the love he felt with Dad was still there, connecting him to Love. This was his Center.

Then it dawned on him. Gay men rarely feel accepted by straight men, let alone one who can touch them with the compassion borne of one who knows the love of a father. He realized in that moment that what he perceived in his clients was actually their need to connect with someone who knew how to connect to men from the heart. Roger's receptors had been cultur-ally conditioned to see affection from gay men as a sexual come-on, when his compassionate touch had simply awakened their need for heart connection, maybe even a heart connection to a man who wasn't their sexual partner. In someone longing for this kind of connection, an attraction to a therapist often gets experienced by the louder *urge-to-merge* receptors, an inability to perceive the difference between the attrac-tion or longing of the heart, from the physical one. When Roger went back to work, his anxiety around working with gay men had decreased, and so did his experience of being pursued by them. The increased comfort in his heart zone may also have helped his clients bring their hearts more in balance with their genitals.

Roger was working in alignment with nature in a couple of ways. He was able to let go of his previous impression of what was happening in the sessions, like cells that let go of genetic informa-tion in order to create something new with another cell. Roger reconnected with parts of himself that had been cut off from his aware-ness, in order to create a new outcome for his clients and himself, thereby differentiating the dimensions of sexual consciousness. The energy he brought to his sessions no longer carried fear or the need to control the sexual sensations in his clients; instead, he brought a heart energy that could touch the heart wounds of his clients. He brought his concerns to me in consultation, engaging another in the complex relationship system for support, which leads us to our next guideline from nature's way with sex.

Place the presenting issue in the context of the larger relationship system of which you're a part.

Roger, by coming to me for supervision, expanded the relationship field in which the sexual energy was moving. In connecting to his father as well as the issues related to the challenges of being gay in our culture, he acknowledged the even larger web of relationship affected by what was happening with his gay clients. Mature ecosys-tems had evolved complex relationship systems around sexuality, and Roger used his capacity for self-awareness and compassion to more consciously engage the larger web of which he and his clients were a part. Let's digress a little here to look at one particular niche in a mature ecosystem to get a better idea of the complexity nature evolved around sex.

A particular flower in the tallgrass prairie ecosystem doesn't produce the nectar which signals its readiness for sex until it hears the song of a particular bird which migrates over the prairie. The flower's nectar-producing cell membrane receptors respond to only that vibra-tional message. The bird's migration is timed to when the particular insect that pollinates that flower is emerging from its pupa (cocoon) stage, and even then the ground conditions have to be right. Quite a few cell membrane receptors have to be working in synchrony to pull this off, the timing has to be exact and not just any bird or insect will turn this flower on. When we act from the knowledge that the sexual issues which present themselves in our healing partnerships exist within a complex web of relationships, and that a successful healing outcome depends on meeting the conditions of that larger system, we foster the maturation of our species around sexuality.

Working with the awareness of the interconnected web of which we're a part can look as simple as recognizing that our actions with individual healing partners reflect on our institutions, professions and communities. It would have helped Lance to realize the larger family system he was touching with Sheila. Oneness helps us see that more than one person's sexual issues are brought into treatment, and what happens in our sessions impacts more than the two of us. Remember, we're working with nature's creative power when sexual issues are present, so the impact of our response carries more potency.

Responding to Unwanted Sexual Advances

By following the five-step process and the guidelines just described, you should be increasingly able to respond skillfully to the sexual issues that present themselves in your healing relationships. However, because I get so many requests from people, especially in the bodywork community, about how to respond to unwanted sexual advances from clients, I offer these more specific suggestions for those circumstances. Unwanted sexual advances usually come from an undifferentiated consciousness or a wound that is ready to come into awareness. They can be quite uncomfortable or even threatening to the practitioner. In our responses, we can both protect ourselves and expand awareness if we follow the cell membrane principles.

Take care of yourself first.

It may be obvious, but it's really okay to protect yourself from a threatening or uncomfortable situation. Cells do it all the time, and that's why animals have immune systems, teeth and claws. I've known therapists who are afraid to deny uncomfortable requests or actions because either they don't feel strong enough to say "no" or they don't know how to. You can simply name your receptors, "I'm uncomfortable (or not prepared, trained) with what you're asking." Or, "I'm uncomfortable with what's happening right now (you can describe what you're observing) and I therefore prefer to end this session." Or, "I notice you keep touching me in a way that feels . . . If you can't contain your feelings and cease touching me, I will have to end the session." As I've said before, with practice, you'll get to where you can respond genuinely from your own empowered Center, without shrinking in fear or judging the request. In case of a forceful advance, it's helpful to know ahead of time how you can terminate the session and seek safety. This is where fear is an ally. Healing is never served when one partner submits to something hurtful; it's always served when you support your own container.

Check out what's happening.

Because sex comes in so many dimensions, emotions and forms of expression, and they mean something different to everyone, it's important to check out what's really intended with a touch of the hand or suggestive comment before assuming it's a sexual advance. If someone asks for a hug, for example, check out how comfortable you are with that and be honest in your response. I know different professions have different rules around touch, but I think the important thing is not whether or not to touch, but clarifying the intention it carries for both of you. You can say things like, "I notice you're often reaching out to touch me and I'm wondering what it is you're wanting." This can help your partner clarify his/her intent. S/he may actually want to get together physically or quite possibly just wants reassurance or comfort. You can respond authentically when you listen to what your receptors are saying and make a conscious choice about what to say or do. Remember, to the extent possible, it's important not to re-energize sexual wounds with a judgmental response or an emotionally distancing one.

Sometimes a client may simply be telling you she wants to get to know you on a personal level, or may even have profound feelings of love for you. This situation can be very delicate, requiring anything but a canned response. Here it's important to reflect what you've heard, and to communicate from your heart that her feelings are important to you in some way. If you jump out of the

183

personal dimension by coldly stating this is a professional relationship and you're not available for a personal one, your partner can easily feel that her heart expression is unacceptable or inappropriate. When someone has shared something from his or her heart, no matter how unwelcome or uncomfortable it may be, it's important to respond from Center while staying connected to your heart.

Be prepared to be wrong.

As I've often said in this book, a receptor or particular set of receptors is conditioned by the quality (wavelength) of messages they've received from others. Often a message similar (same general wavelength) to the message that tuned the receptor in the first place can trigger a conditioned response, like Sheila's response to Lance's touch. If your personal sexual story carried messages of mistrust of the opposite sex, you're more likely to respond in fear or judgment to an action that actually isn't a threat or advance at all. When you're a nail, everything looks like a hammer. I've known several instances when actions from clients trigger a "Not with me you won't!" response in a therapist, when the client's intention was far from what the therapist thought it was. As I said above, if you check out what's really happening with your partner, what he says can then become the focus of the response. For example, if your partner answers your inquiry about touching you by saying, "I just want to show you how much I appreciate you," you can focus your response on his appreciation. Take him at his word by saying, "It's nice to be appreciated, but it will be easier for me to focus on (whatever his healing need is) if I'm not being touched." In this way, you're responding to what he actually says instead of your projected fear. Should he persist in touching you, you could draw attention to it again and inquire further about what he is doing. It draws his attention to what he's doing (containment) and what he's actually doing serves as the basis for whether you continue the session, not your projection. By staying tuned to your own receptors while you check out what's happening in your partner, you can contain the behavior and feeling to prevent discomforting energy from flowing into interspace.

Lighten up.

Collectively, we professionals have gotten so intense around issues of sexuality in healing, that sometimes a little humor can disperse some of the anxiety and create a healthy shift in the energy. Humor brings light to anxiety—as long as it comes from the heart or Center and not the need to control out of fear. Without diminishing either the power or the seriousness of sexual issues, sometimes a light-hearted comment can clear interspace as much as a confrontation. If someone is becoming personally attracted to you, or is feeling sexually aroused during a session, it doesn't have to be a big, serious deal—it's just what's happening. There's no need to do anything about it. This can be a challenge, especially if you've been conditioned to put up boundaries every time something uncomfortable happens. Practice with the cell membrane principles will help you eventually allow potentially discomforting messages to just be in interspace without reacting to them.

Work on your own sexual longings and wounds.

This suggestion re-emphasizes the importance of getting intimate with the sexual stories held in your receptors. It also underscores the role your own receptors play as magnets for the kind of experiences you have with clients. Your longing, for example, can attract just the situation in a session that brings that longing into consciousness.

> *Temptation is the magnet which draws your awareness to that which would create negative karma if it were allowed to remain unconscious.*
>
> — *Gary Zukov*

When I need to awaken to fears or desires I don't know I have, someone always shows up to trigger them. Usually, when I encounter something difficult in a session, sexually or otherwise, it leads me to something I need to look at about my own receptors. If you're attracting a particular kind of sexual situation or feelings, like Roger was with his gay clients, the more you clear your own wounds, the less likely it will be that they appear in your sessions. This isn't placing the blame for a situation on the person feeling threatened—blaming the victim—or saying you're creating the attraction with your wounds. According to the cell membrane model both partners contribute to what happens between them. Unhealthy sexual feelings and behaviors are prevalent in our culture and touch all of us, so everything we do to transform our own wounds can affect those we work with. I've had women students who have been

---

Keys to Healing Responses to Unwanted Sexual Advances

- **Take Care of Yourself First**
- **Check out What's Happening**
- **Be Prepared to Be Wrong**
- **Lighten Up**
- **Work on Your Own Sexual Longings and Wounds**

---

so traumatized sexually that they encounter some really offensive and threatening behaviors from their clients. Offensive and threatening behaviors are not limited to men, of course, but if a woman feels threatened around men, she may want to restrict her practice to women until she feels safe.

Resonance is a powerful process that can bypass the conscious mind. You can tell yourself that you've worked through and healed your sexual wounds, and set very clear boundaries with your clients, but resonance will take you to the next stop on your psychospiritual journey. By just being able to look at the situations you encounter in your healing relationships as a function of resonance— not judgment—you can be better prepared to select and be more conscious of what you let in and out of your personal space. If you've been deeply wounded sexually, taking a firm stand about what you will and will not do can be profoundly healing for you and your healing partners.

Overall, the more you can bring your partner's awareness to what he's doing and saying, the more you are helping him to contain and increase his awareness of his sexual process. If what he's doing or saying is offensive or threatening to you, if you can connect to and respond from Center, what you say and place in interspace will serve healing, even if it makes him uncomfortable. I once had to tell a client that what he was doing, which I spelled out, was frightening me. He was offended that I should react in such a way, but he eventually assumed responsibility for his actions and thanked me for making him aware of the feelings that drove his aggressive action.

When the Attraction is Mutual

I summarized the last chapter by saying that dual relationships demand a high level of self-awareness to avoid the pitfalls and mine the potential of such relationships. This is especially true when sexual energy is involved. As I've indicated throughout this book, more often than not, a strong—and even mutual—sexual attraction between healing partners usually points to a resonance around an issue asking for attention. Because the projection process can be so compelling in healing relationships, it's easy to experience your partner as the ideal lover or mate. Everything about your healing partner seems perfect—especially because she thinks you're so wonderful! The relationship has allowed each of you to open to parts of yourself you didn't know were there, and the intimacy that results from being allowed inside someone's innermost process can easily be mistaken for the kind of love you've longed for all your life. If you become profoundly attracted to your healing partner, and you've tried to follow nature's guidelines toward a skillful response, what do you do if the attraction persists? If you sense in your heart that your partner feels the same way—what would the cell membrane have you do?

Professional codes of ethics, while very clear in their intent to prevent harm, offer little guidance about how to skillfully respond to such a mutual attraction. They function in the power and control dimension of sexuality, leaving practitioners with few options other than abstinence or defiance. The five-step process described in Chapter 9 together with the navigational skills outlined in the chapter on dual relationships invite *consciousness expansion* around what's been activated by the relationship. In short, is it possible for you to track, contain and support your partner's process and your own and work from Center in the relationship? If not, then it's best to discontinue the healing relationship. But what if you find that you are able to contain your desires and work from Center to your partner's benefit, what then?

Some codes of ethics require that you terminate the professional relationship before starting a personal one; some even prescribe a specific waiting period. Who is to know what's a reasonable time for most people regardless of circumstance? I've observed instances where the waiting period merely heightened the attraction and did nothing to help the partners increase their awareness of what is driving the sexual attraction. While I support the idea of taking time apart to tease out the projections and transference, it's also important to seek counsel from a trusted colleague or supervisor. Supervision expands the relationship system and helps you gain a larger perspective on what's happening. Healing partners who are prepared to engage in that level of self-inquiry may be capable of a sexual healing relationship, but not likely a professional one. Remember how in mature natural systems all conditions have to be right for sex. In those rare circumstances where a healing relationship leads to a deep and abiding love, that love survives and is enriched by the consciousness raising that nature asks of us around sexuality.

Plants and animals have evolved to take themselves through quite an elaborate selectivity process when it comes to sexuality, and we can evolve to do the same. I don't pretend to fully understand nature's way with sex, which continues to evolve as I write and you read. However, the principles outlined in this book offer both the personal and professional responsibility that codes of ethics strive for, while giving us the flexibility and creativity that nature intends around sexuality. Let's move now into how the sexual maturity gained from that kind of inquiry can help us be a more healing presence for someone who has been sexually traumatized.

Healing Presence with Sexual Trauma

> *I am the 12-year-old girl, refugee on a small boat,*
>
> *who throws herself into the ocean after being raped by a sea pirate,*
>
> *and I am the pirate, my heart not yet capable of seeing and loving.*
>
> —*Thich Nhat Hanh*

Sexual wounding is particularly potent because it leaves a creative outcome in its wake—an outcome that carries the intention of the perpetrator into the future, into the body of its victim and into the interspace that touches all of us. Sexual wounding survives even death as it weaves its way into our sexual stories and shapes the sexual receptors that get carried into the next generation.

Skillful and caring response to those who suffer from sexual trauma helps to heal the sexual wounds that affect our whole human family. It's beyond the scope of this book to try to show you how to specifically help someone heal sexual trauma, but the cell membrane that manages nature's sexual relationships can help you recognize sexual trauma and be a more compassionate presence when you encounter it in your practice.

Sexual abuse occurs whenever sexual energy is used to breach and penetrate the physical or psychospiritual container of another person with the unhealed wounds of the perpetrator. Because of its creative power, sexual energy adds potency to any emotional vibration it carries. When a sexual encounter carries the feelings of love, for example, the love grows, even beyond the two

189

people involved. Conversely, when someone is raped, sexual energy carries the vibration of anger, self-loathing or powerlessness of the perpetrator into the being of the victim. It has an even greater impact on the victim than if the perpetrator's self-loathing or powerlessness was acted out in a non-sexual way. Sexual abuse can be as obvious as rape or as subtle as the missteps of therapists who are unable to contain their own sexual feelings with their clients. Whether we've directly experienced sexual abuse, read or seen it in the news, or felt it in the body of the person we're working with, we feel it deeply because it violates something so innately precious to life.

The physical, mental, emotional and spiritual effects of sexual abuse and trauma present themselves in a myriad of symptoms in our healing partners. In my work with people suffering from chronic pain or illness, anxiety, depression, or relationship problems, sexual trauma often surfaces in connection to the particular symptom that brought them to treatment. So we don't have to be sexual trauma specialists to respond compassionately and skillfully to issues of sexual wounding that surface unexpectedly in a healing partner's work with us. Those wounds are often unknown to our healing partners until they begin working with the presenting symptom.

The younger someone is when they are sexually abused, the more holistic the harm to their development, i.e. it affects all dimensions of their being. A fetus, infant or very young child can't differentiate the physical from the psychological or spiritual dimensions of the sexual spectrum. If their conception and gestation was accompanied by sexual misuse of the mother, the energy of that misuse creatively imbeds itself in the developing tissue and psyche of the fetus. When we're born, we still feel at one with all we sense in our earthly environment. Until we begin to differentiate, first physically, then emotionally and mentally, from our immediate environment, our receptors are profoundly influenced by the actions and feelings of our parents. The home environment forms the foundation of our experience of life in this body. Abuse creates distrust and a deep longing in the whole being of the child to connect in a healthy way to others. Yet often, in those abused so young, the abusive behaviors shape their receptors around all relationships. If touch and nurture were associated with the abuse, touch and nurture are likely to be experienced in subsequent relationships as abusive, or something close to abuse.

While I have had professional training specifically in healing trauma, as well as in sexual abuse, it's been my healing partners who have taught me the most about the profound effect of sexual abuse on growth and development. It's through them that the full-spectrum of consciousness about sexuality made itself so visible. Through them I learned how pervasively sexual abuse underlies so many of our common chronic diseases. Healing partners also taught me about the potential for healing that arises when the wounded receptors are transformed by awareness and compassionate presence. When a therapist can accompany the abuse survivor through all the dimensions of her sexual wounds and stay Centered while doing so, healing can happen without needing to do much more than be compassionately present with your partner as she faces her pain. This is where the cell membrane model has helped the most as I practice the principles of containment, selective permeability, inter-space, differentiation, centering and Oneness with these healing partners.

Sexual trauma hides out in so many body systems, psychological processes and relationship problems that it's impossible to list for you all the symptoms that indicate you are working with a deep sexual wound. If you're familiar with family systems theories or transpersonal psychology, it will come as no surprise that the abuse didn't even have to have happened to the individual you're working with to manifest as a disease or a symptom of sexual imbalance and wounding. A family pattern, which is unconsciously supported by the entire family system, can present itself for healing several generations later under the right conditions, the right healing relationship. If you work with past-life regressions, you're familiar with those who work out and heal the present body of sexual wounds from a previous incarnation. So, it's not that you should be looking for sexual trauma underneath every symptomatic stone, but be accepting of what surfaces in your sessions and be prepared to let the cell membrane model help you move with ease through co-creative healing without further traumatizing your partner. The following guidelines can help you respond the way the cell membrane would ask you to.

What you see may not be what you think it is.

Seductive behavior in a client may be only the tip of an iceberg, the base of which is sexual abuse. The adult you see may have regressed into a traumatized child who was taught what she had to do in order to receive acceptance. A man making an advance may be acting out the need for reassurance of his manhood, which was cruelly threatened or humiliated as a boy. Remember, the wounds of our cultural sexual stories can show up in strange ways in our treatment spaces. Sexual arousal or expressions of joy could be portals to sexual pain, as we saw with Sheila. Rather than help Sheila bring greater awareness to her body and what it holds, Lance inadvertently triggered a trauma. It's important to just witness what's happening, in you and your partner, trusting that containment will enhance awareness of what's happening inside, that is, which receptors are waking up. Rather than react to what you see and feel, it's always better to work with containment and support, to Center yourself so that interspace holds nothing but the compassion these wounded receptors often need.

A situation comes to mind that illustrates the need to not react to what you see, but contain the process. I once worked with a woman in an aquatic session who began to bat her eyes at me as she wriggled up close. As her face suddenly changed expression, I tracked and contained without reacting. She batted her eyes again and asked me what I wanted in a very seductive way. I sensed then that she had psychologically regressed to a childhood state; I knew how important it was to not react, but to just remain centered and respond with compassion. Eventually she pleaded that if she didn't please me sexually, she would get punished. I gently told her that I didn't need any sexual contact with her. When her eyes narrowed in fear, I assured her that I wouldn't hurt her. She continued to be seductive, but I met every seductive move with centered compassion, always assuring her that she was safe. Eventually the energy of the trauma, met in such a way, was able to shift and the seductive behavior ended.

Imagine the trauma to this woman if I had either allowed her to touch me sexually or responded in a way that carried judgment of her "inappropriate" behavior. I had to just contain and support her process, while staying centered in my own. Of course, throughout the course of treatment with this woman, I employed other therapeutic approaches (see reference section) as well, to help her heal from the trauma, but the foundation for my work was the cell membrane model.

You don't have to do anything.

Just meeting sexual trauma with your own compassionate presence when it reveals itself is the most healing thing you can do. Your own discomfort around what you've heard or seen often makes you want to say or do something to help your partner understand or feel better, or make the terrible feelings go away. I remember one of the first times a woman I worked with entered into a body memory of sexual abuse. I was so horrified by what she said, that I said to myself, "You don't know how to deal with this." And I didn't. But there she was, so my only tool was my heart. I just stayed beside her in witness to her pain. I didn't ask any questions, offer interpretation or advice, or flood interspace with my need to make her pain go away. It's not easy to do, because you start feeling the fear and betrayal floating in interspace and it touches similar receptors in you. But Centering and Oneness usually help me find the compassion to just hold space for the healing partner's process. It's the most powerful aspect of any intervention I can recommend.

It's the truth.

The trust that enables your partner to enter a memory of sexual trauma will be lost immediately, and the wound re-energized, when you question the validity of what you're hearing from the client. Sexually traumatized people have highly refined receptors around people doubting the truth of their experience. Even if you suspect that what they're saying or experiencing is a projection or adaptive fantasy and not fact, their experience of it is true, and that's what you're there to witness. You're in a healing, not investigative relationship, and as long as what happens between you stays within the healing relationship container, it's not going to do damage to someone they might be accusing of sexual abuse. I've found that to the extent someone is able to contain, but express what they're feeling, the internal healing process clarifies and integrates what's been revealed without any need to investigate or take further action.

I recall clients who initially reported things that sounded so preposterous, I thought they just couldn't be true, only to find amazing correlations and internal validity with revelations throughout subsequent sessions. We hear a lot about "false memories," and the research is anything but conclusive. However, the selective permeability, interspace and containment principles of the cell membrane model tell us that we can observe the information we hear in interspace and either take in the subjective experience of that information or not. When we employ containment and keep our judgment out of interspace, we support our partner's experience of what's been said. Their energy field, mind and body hold the truth of the experience, which is where we can affect a shift with awareness, trust and compassion.

Try not to run away.

There are so many ways to run away from what's uncomfortable. Withdrawal through quality of touch or voice can be excruciating to someone who has just revealed something they may not have even acknowledged to themselves before. People who have been sexually abused, especially in childhood, have been silenced and distanced from because those around them simply cannot handle what they share. Their receptors know all the subtle ways folks, especially those who profess to want to help them, distance themselves in protection. A healing partner once challenged all the professionally correct things I was saying in such a way that he enabled me to see through the mask I was wearing—I was trying to get away. When I admitted to both of us how tough it was for me to face his pain over and over again, we were able to set the frequency of our sessions in a way that honestly honored my capacity without distancing myself from him. I agreed to try to be more sensitive to when my receptors were reaching capacity before I unconsciously distanced. We realized I simply didn't have enough receptors to handle the intensity of what he was sending, not that what he was sending was too much. Can you see the subtle difference? Over time, my receptors grew in capacity, but when they were full, I'd just say so and he understood that we were limited by how much I could handle, not that he's too much—which is what he had heard all his life.

Many of the boundary setting practices we use mask our need to run away or distance ourselves. It's not that we shouldn't set limits on our capacity, or on what we are and are not prepared for, but it's helpful to these partners, who have experienced so much abandonment, to be more specific about which of our receptors we're acting from and when. Rather than setting broad, unyielding boundaries, we can engage our partners in co-creating the limits. Even though our intention is to provide structure for partners who lack structure, it's important to realize that those whose whole being was so creatively assaulted need to hold some of the building blocks with which the new structure is built. This is delicate work, but it gives you the chance to tune into your own receptors about what you really need, and trust your partners to honor your containment.

Follow your pain inside.

When discomfort that arose in a session stays with you afterward, it can lead you into greater awareness and compassion. The five-step process can take you there, and of course it can be adapted to the specific occasion. Once, after a healing partner revealed her experience of sexual abuse, she quietly asked, "How could someone do such a thing to another human being?" Of course, I had no answer. That night I awoke in a very irritable state and couldn't fall back to sleep. Giving up, I went to the living room, put on a piece of music (see Resources) that helps me work through different emotional states, releasing them through movement. Thoughts of my client were far out of my mind, so by moving I only hoped to release the irritability and get back to sleep. As I moved through a portion of the music, my inner vision served up an image, or more like a felt experience, of myself torturing someone. I was crushing someone's head under my boot and really feeling high about it! My witness self could hardly believe what I was experiencing, but the vision persisted. As I kept moving, the high gave way to deep remorse, which intensified until the feelings suddenly shifted again. I felt compassion and Love flowing into every cell of my body, awareness bigger and brighter than I'd experienced before—as powerful as the high I was feeling as a torturer. Now, I don't know and it doesn't seem to matter, whether this was a memory of a past life or whether I was tapping into a collective consciousness, but I couldn't deny that I had a receptor that knew the pleasure of hurting another human being. The experience helped reinforce my understanding that the shadow and light parts of us hang out together inside. When I can meet and accept the shadow, the light is right there too, ready to integrate and evolve into a new relationship or understanding. The differentiation and oneness principles were operable here to enable me to bring more compassion to my work, which brings us to the issue of working with those we either know have abused others or suspect that they have.

"Call me by my many names."

This is another phrase in the poem I partially quoted at the beginning of this chapter by Thich Nhat Hanh, a Buddhist monk who witnessed all manner of suffering as a young man in war-torn Vietnam. He now brings his message of compassion to millions all over the world through his teachings and workshops. He has helped U. S. Viet Nam War veterans return to the places where they either witnessed or perpetrated trauma during the war. He couldn't have done this work if he hadn't learned to embrace both the raped and the rapist and see the Oneness in us all.

We don't all have to be Buddhist monks to learn to be compassionate to those who harm others. It's one thing to know, understand and even talk about the power of compassion and the need for forgiveness, but another to embody it. It took that experience in my living room, where I felt both the thrill and the remorse of the harm I was capable of inflicting, to more fully embody compassion.

Remorse is excruciating, but every time I'm forced by circumstances or my inner process to feel it throughout my body, remorse becomes a portal to healing. Guilt, on the other hand, is a paralyzing emotion; it keeps us stuck in judgment. By moving into and through remorse I'm better able to respond more skillfully when I'm faced with the realization that someone I trust or work with has harmed another. I've been there—I've hurt others.

Yet, because I've witnessed the pervasive effects of sexual abuse in my healing partners, at times I still find it difficult to be compassionate when I hear of someone sexually abusing another. Then I remember the eyes of Michael, a father of four children whom I supervised in foster care in my first social work practicum. I'll never forget him. Michael committed heinous sexual abuse of these children, either directly or by the abusive energy he contributed to the family interspace. When I read the case history, I nearly got sick—it took a while to get through it. I wasn't looking forward to supervising a visit that the agency scheduled for him and his children. I didn't want to see such a man who could do this to children, children I had grown to love.

Well, Michael wasn't the monster I imagined. The pain in his eyes, his slumped shoulders, rough and weathered skin and overall countenance revealed not a monster, but a beaten man. I watched as he hesitated, reaching out to just say hi to his children. His shame was palpable, and I saw how his children carried the shame as well. The love among them was palpable too, revealing a paradox I've never fully understood, but have come to embrace. It's possible to both love and grievously wound at the same time. I was powerless to do anything other than witness the scene before me. Was I ready to recommend the children return to his home? Not at all—so much more healing was needed. I never learned how it all turned out, but if I were to work with him—and I've subsequently worked with some people who've abused others—I would look to the cell membrane to guide me. It would guide me to contain my reaction to what I saw, follow my pain inside for release and transformation, and help him to contain his awareness of what he'd done. I'd try to help him follow his pain inside, and believe what he told me, while not ascrib-

197

ing it as fact. I would try to hold all he was in interspace and help us find our way to Center to wait for the light of Love to touch us both in Oneness. Selective permeability would let me know what was triggered by what I witnessed in him, and help me decide how to share that with him in interspace; from Center I would seek a response that would help him expand his understanding of his own life and how what he was doing was affecting his children.

You might ask what I would have done if he'd been belligerent or offensive to his children during the visit. I would do what I could to contain his belligerence within his own field, and take the children to safety. They were the most vulnerable and I was charged with their protection. A man like Michael may never reach the awareness needed to work on his own healing, but by protecting his children I would have given his receptors an opportunity to possibly see something different than his former life experience had allowed—to offer some differentiation energy to his mix. Several weeks after I supervised that visit, our staff was given an in-service on research that profiled adults who sexually abuse children. The research overwhelmingly supported the impression of what I saw in Michael's eyes. The more severe the abuse, the more powerless the abuser; the less able he is to know and feel his own pain so that he doesn't inflict it on others. There are other characteristics as well, none of which support the impression that he's a monster, just a severely wounded man. Men and women who are genuinely grounded in their own power, and feel accepted by and connected to others in relationship, don't rape children.

A Word to Men

Men aren't the only sexual abusers, nor have they been spared from sexual abuse, especially if we espouse nature's paradigm for sexuality and the Oneness of all life. Yet men in the helping professions are accused of sexual abuse far more often than women, and the cultural sexual stories that place men in control of women perpetuate the cycle of abuse. Ironically, because so many women and children have been sexually abused by men, those men who can embody the cell membrane model are in a unique position to provide co-creative healing. As we saw with Lance, however, it takes a tremendous amount of inner-awareness and self-healing for a man to be able to be fully present with a woman who has been hurt by the touch of a man. The careers of many well-meaning men have been shattered by charges of sexual misconduct. Here are a few tips you can follow in addition to the natural principles listed above and throughout this book:

Assume the woman or child you are working with has been sexually abused.

This may sound outrageous, but statistics tell us that at least 30 percent of all women have—and that's just counting reportable abuse that is usually pretty severe or illegal. It doesn't count the abuse hidden in women with chronic illness or emotional or psychological problems that haven't yet surfaced into their awareness—or even in women who have no symptoms. It doesn't count the models whose bodies have been starved so they look good to 11 million viewers as they walk down the runway in a bra and panties, or all those other women whose bodies have been exploited to sell something. It doesn't count the women who grew up thinking that all a man wants is to get in your pants. If the woman in your treatment space has grown up with the messages of rape in war and worldwide oppression of women flashing across her TV set and in the movies, her receptors have been tuned

---

Guidelines for Healing Presence when Working with Sexual Abuse Survivors

- **What you see may not be what you think it is.**
- **You don't have to do anything.**
- **It's the truth.**
- **Try not to run away.**
- **Follow your pain inside.**

to be wary of men. When a woman running for President of the United States gets pelted by sexually demeaning epithets, or a misogynist former Attorney General covers the breasts on the statues outside the United States Department of Justice, all women are hurt. The degree of sexual abuse varies a whole lot, but the Oneness principle and my experience with women has shown me that it's impossible for us not to be deeply wounded by the abuse that's so prevalent in modern life.

My point here is not about how much or what kind of abuse women have experienced, but to heighten your awareness about the nature of the sexual receptors you're likely to encounter in your healing practice. The receptors in women who have suffered abuse can pick up the slightest vibration from you of any intention other than a healing or compassionate one. As I mentioned earlier—what you see may not be all there is, and wounds that neither of you know are there have receptors that can read and react to any non-healing intention you send into interspace.

It's important to note also that men suffer from the exploitation of women. The Oneness principle tells us that we hurt ourselves when we hurt others. In men this can be experienced as an alienation from their emotional and spiritual selves. Their wounded sexual receptors color all aspects of their relationships to women, and everyone suffers.

Some signs to look for

Lest you feel you need to be excessively cautious around all women, there are some indicators in a woman's behavior that signal a need to move slowly and pay close attention to what's happening in you and in your partner. All of these behaviors, of course, do not mean someone is a survivor of severe sexual abuse, or that someone who doesn't exhibit these behaviors is not; rather, the behavior itself warrants more awareness on your part.

- *Your partner appears frightened, extremely shy or with - drawn.* Your approach with such a woman needs to be slow, genuinely caring and respectful of her personal space.

Probing questions or suggestions that she "relax" will feel like an invasion. Hold her anxiety in interspace without the need to reflect her behavior back to her in any way. You are doing your best to create a safe space with just your presence. Moves toward treatment are to be taken very slowly and with compassion. Even if you end up doing very little, the trust that builds between you will form the foundation of the relationship.

- *Your partner acts very seductive or "open" to whatever you want to do.* This situation as well calls for moving slowly with containment and connection to your Center. Like the situation I described earlier when the woman had regressed to childhood, playing along with the seduction or judging it in any way will re-energize sexual wounds at best, re-traumatize at worst.

- *Your partner sets particularly defensive or rigid boundaries.* On the path to healing, many women whose personal space has been violated sexually learn to set firm boundaries, an important first step and one that needs to be supported until she gains the skill to work with the selectivity and differentiation of the cell membrane model. If you sense fear or anxiety as she sets her boundaries, verbally or through body language, hold your compassion at the edge of that boundary, without trying to budge it in any way. Just be there, and proceed sensitively and with awareness.

- *Your partner shows no regard for her personal space and has no boundaries.* This situation isn't always easy to assess, but repeated statements like, "I don't know" or "It doesn't matter" suggest someone who doesn't feel in charge of her personal space or even her life. Another manifestation of this presents itself as a willingness or need to merge with you, a sense that she loses herself in your presence, attributing all kinds of healing or spiritual powers to you. There's a fine line between being willing to let go of what's no longer serving her in order to create something new, and having no personal identity to start with, only the need to fuse emotionally with another.

All of the above behaviors can trigger some of your own receptors, and this is where tracking, containment and support of your self are important. In general, when your partner's focus is either on you and what you are doing, or so withdrawn into herself that she can't connect with you in any way, you can assume that her ability to connect for co-creative work is impaired by some kind of personal wounding, and often that's sexual.

Sometimes a woman doesn't exhibit any of the above behaviors and is able to connect with you in a co-creative way. When hersexual wounds can be met by a man who is able to stay centered in compassion, the trust in the relationship creates the safe space in which she can face these issues. Gradually, she discovers power in her own growing awareness and capacity to heal, not in the therapist's power to do it for her.

Be very clear about your motives and intentions with each healing partner.

Men who abuse women and children often accompany the abuse with expressions of wanting to take care of them or protect them. When the abused woman's receptors perceive a *therapist's need* to *take care* of her or *his* need to make her feel safe, it is possible that she could associate that message with the abuse. Doesn't seem fair, does it, to the guy who just wants to help? Some perpetrators needed to feel their power or manhood by abusing women. Therefore, any vibrational hint of a need to feel good about yourself as a man by helping women will get picked up by those sensitive wounded receptors of your partner. Even though Lance was motivated by a genuine desire to help women appreciate themselves, he did so out of *his* need to help Sheila; to Sheila his need felt just like Daddy's need for her. This is admittedly very tough and challenges your ability to track and contain your own feelings and motivations and work from Center. It's tricky because the line between being caring, protective or helpful and *needing* to do these things is often hard to find.

I've been very impressed by male therapists who have worked hard to get to know their own sexual receptors, who have tracked their hidden desires, longings and intentions, and have consequently been extremely helpful and healing with women. After working with a sexual abuse survivor for a period of time, I often will refer her to one of these men because I know their compassionate touch and presence can be so healing. Interspace is clear of his fears, longings or desires and safe for holding those of his partner.

Be aware of the Rescuer/Victim/Perpetrator triangle.

If a woman looks to you to rescue her or be her savior in any way, both of you, almost without realizing it, can fall into a situation in which the roles shift. The woman begins to experience her rescuer as the perpetrator—taking her back to a time when rescuer and perpetrator were both in control of her. In reaction to yet another situation in which she's powerless, she might say you've crossed her boundary, or even bring charges of ethical misconduct—and you become the victim. In healing relationships caught in this triangle, both people can move from one position to another almost unconsciously and in subtle ways. The therapist who follows the cell membrane model with regard to power and control, knows that the power for healing must be balanced between them. As long as both the practitioner and his partner attribute the success or failure of the treatment to only what he does, they both get stuck in the rescuer-victim-perpetrator triangle.

It's important to remember—whether you are a man or a woman—that you can't erase thousands of years of abuse to women on your own. "Sexual saviors," those who want to be the ones to heal the sexual wounds of women, often get trapped in this triangle. Women usually like and initially feel very safe with these therapists, but once deep into the therapy, those "savior" messages in interspace begin to feel painfully familiar and the old trauma is triggered. Again, it's important to check out the perceived power differential between you and your partner, and what you each think about who is responsible for the healing.

Touch with sensitivity, awareness and permission.

If your healing modality doesn't involve touch, as in psychotherapy, for instance, make sure you're very clear on your motive and that you've either sensed that your touch is welcome or you've asked permission to touch her. When you ask, make sure you're really asking, not just going through the automatic, professional process—the energy in your voice will tell her the difference.

If touch is part of your modality, the more you can develop the ability to sense even the most subtle tissue or emotional response to your touch, the better able you'll be to respond in a healing way and not have your touch be felt as abuse. Touch requires a keenly developed sensitivity to nuance and body language, and even an ability to communicate with the unconscious parts of your partner. When your approach carries a non-verbal message asking permission to touch, you are less likely to trigger abuse receptors than if you abruptly start touching. You can also ask your partner from time to time about how the work is feeling, if the pressure is right, etc. Even the angle at which you move your hand or fingers can make a difference in how the touch is received. A sensitive woman can pick up if you're directing the touch toward her or responding to an invitation. I know, too, that connecting your awareness to your intention as you touch can make a lot of difference in helping your partner feel safe.

Notice repeating patterns.

When you repeatedly hear from women that "you're so wonderful" or "no one has ever touched me (or listened, or acted) like that before" or "you've changed my life," you may begin to ask yourself where the power in the relationship lies. Are you really doing the women a service if they still attribute the power for how they feel to the man they're with. Again, we're talking fine lines. It's very important for women who have been wounded by men to finally trust someone, to feel heard and cared for and to be able to express gratitude for it. But we're talking degree of ownership of the healing process here, and the frequency with which you hear these and similar phrases offers you a clue. Check in with your own receptors about how important (or irritating) it has become for you to hear this repeatedly. No need to become less wonderful, but it may be time to look at what you're contributing to the power imbalance.

Similarly, you may go through a period where you are attracting any number of difficult relationship challenges with women—you can't please them, or nothing seems to work, or they don't seem to trust you. Conversely, you find yourself becoming sexually attracted to women over and over again. Repeating patterns like this suggest that work on your relationships with women is indicated.

~~~

Male therapists who can be fully present with women as they heal from sexual abuse not only help their particular healing partners, but they also contribute to the development of healthy and mature gender relationships in the culture. Women who have experienced the presence and conscious touch of such a therapist are far less likely to allow themselves to be touched in any other way again. Their receptors will no longer serve as magnets for abuse, and the effect will act like a pebble gently tossed into the pond.

A Word to Women

When women therapists can wrap their minds around the fact that men have been equally wounded by the sexually abusive environment we live in, their responses to the men who come to them for healing can foster cultural healing as well. Women can look to all I've said in my "word to men" and transpose it to fit the situations they encounter with male healing partners. It's important to remember that men also carry the receptors formed by our old sexual stories about what it means to be a man and who has the power in a relationship. It's equally true that many men now are consciously working to retune their receptors so that they can live a more fulfilling and co-creative sexual life. I remember working with a man who had so buried his male power under the shame and guilt of what men had done to women over time, that he lost a sense of who he was as a man. We had to slowly and consciously work to excavate those masculine qualities and integrate them with the feminine aspects of his being that he'd been cultivating. As we bring conscious and compassionate care to the sexual issues that arise with our healing partners of both genders, we contribute to the evolution of a new story about sexuality in humans.

An Evolutionary Leap

Nature evolved sexuality to respond creatively to environmental challenges that threatened life as it was, and those very threats spurred the ongoing evolution of life on the planet. I wonder, then, if the prevalence of sexual abuse in cultures all over the world today can be looked at as an opportunity to take the next evolutionary leap.

In Anodea Judith's book, *Waking the Global Heart,* she traces the development of humans in relationship to each other and Earth up to present time. Judith beautifully outlines how we are currently evolving from the "love of power to the power of love." She joins Elisabet Sahtouris and others in calling our attention to the major evolutionary shift now happening on Earth. The central archetype for this awakening, according to Judith, is Partnership. The battle of the sexes will be over, to be replaced by a co-creative partnership based on the self-organizing systems of nature.

We have an enormous opportunity, by being the ones who touch the wounds created by our imbalance with nature, to help our species grow into sexual maturity and foster the evolutionary partnerships that Judith, Sahtouris and others describe. Such partnerships can propel us beyond planetary destruction and into planetary transformation. Sexuality is too precious a gift of nature to be used to create and energize wounds that grow out of relationship models that rest on something other than nature's ground. The cell membrane model for managing relationships and sexuality can guide our healing relationships toward reconnection with the living web in which we all dance.

206

Am I giving sexuality too much power? No, because sexuality fueled life's capacity to literally shape this planet, so our attitudes toward sex can shape our future. No, because evolutionary and systems biologists, historians, philosophers, anthropologists and social scientists are now showing us how our inability to understand and live in alignment with nature's co-creative power has brought us to this point of evolutionary crisis, where life on Earth is at risk. Maybe it's time to let go of life as we know it and foster our evolution to life as it can be. That can start with how you work with life's co-creative power in your treatment space, one healing partnership at a time.

THE JOURNEY ENDS

"My body was reaching back into a cellular experience, of being a water creature, of coming up into the air, and onto the land. I felt as though I reached an even deeper layer of memory, not my own memory, but one that stretched back through my mother, through generation after generation, untold thousands or hundreds of thou - sands of years into the past. I felt as though my own expe - rience of the breath carried this mammalian memory, this message encoded within the simple physical act of the breath, this faint trail that leads back to where we have come from."

— *Karen*

Karen came to me for an aquatic bodywork session while going through a particularly stressful time in her life. Some things had fallen apart and she was unsure of her footing in family and career. It was a beautiful day. The sun shone brightly through the trees to create a lattice of light and shadow on the pool floor. As Karen's body surrendered to the movement and flow in the water, it seemed she was tapping into the healing energy of this ancient site, now called Harbin Hot Springs, which drew me into its vortex as well. The breeze rustled through the pines as the squirrels scurried through the dry leaves, and an occasional deer wandered by, all of us becoming partners in Karen's healing. Karen didn't say much after the session, but it was obvious to me that she had come to a new place in her healing process. Not only had she released muscle tension and some tears into the pool, but upon opening her eyes, she looked so different from when we began. To talk about it at this moment seemed like a breach of containment. Her experience needed to gestate awhile. Knowing that Karen was a writer, I suggested she write about her experience in her journal when the words naturally surfaced and asked for expression. The next day, when she shared what she had written, it seemed we had stepped into the kind of healing relationship I've been describing in these pages. All the elements and principles that we've explored in these pages were there. Years after I began to search through nature's web to discover a new model for ethics in healing relationships, this time with Karen seemed to bring it to completion.

I began this journey at Fort Ross years ago with the questions: What does it take to be fully present with another in the face of illness and pain? What would it take to make the relationship itself the container for healing? Certainly, in the session with Karen, all the cell membrane principles were present to help us create the container in which Karen could expand her awareness of who she was and where she came from and surrender to the flow of life's unfolding in the present moment. Both of us met the receptors that sounded in turn, contained them, and observed what happened in the liquid interspace we shared with the healing environment of Harbin. At some point in the session, however, we shifted into Oneness where Karen could perceive herself in a new way. She wrote in her journal:

> *"This memory is not 'Karen', and yet the end of this particular trail is Karen. Here in this very body is a path toward what lies behind and beyond Karen."*

Even though I didn't know the words of her experience during the session, I did feel the shift in interspace. Everything was quiet, calm and peaceful. Love was there, the same quality of Love that Amber and I felt as we stood in the fading light after she moved through another layer of grief for her daughter's torture and death. It's the Love that is the source of healing power. This relationship with Karen was co-creativity at its best, and I was grateful that my journey into the mystery of the healing relationship had brought us to this awareness. Of course, not all sessions end like that, and I continue to be taken into a deeper exploration of the cell membrane principles every time I face something new and challenging, something that calls for the co-creative impulse that nature offers in time of struggle.

This "particular trail" of writing has come to a close, but I hope as you put these principles to work in your own healing practice, that they take you on an ongoing journey of discovery. As Earth continues its journey, we will be invited into its evolutionary dance in ways I couldn't have imagined in the writing of this book. It's likely that by the time this book reaches you, more about nature's way of relationship will have revealed itself—material I wish I had known, practiced and understood by now. For this reason, I invite you to:

Continue the Journey

The static pages of a book may be insufficient to keep up with the pace of growing and change taking place in healing practices right now. Therefore, I have created some internet resources through which we can communicate and evolve around relationships that heal. Please visit my website at http://www.dianetegtmeier.com for a blog, information about workshops, online courses and a newsletter to engage you in an ongoing exploration of nature's way with relationships. Karen ended her session with this insight, which she shared with me from her journal:

> "The insight flashed within—we are at just such a place, just such an evolutionary fork in the path. What are we in the process of becoming? Where will we evolve from here? If we retreat into fear and doubt, won't we sink back, or worse, erase ourselves from the planetary record? Hopefully we will find the next step that propels us toward an evolutionary leap, toward

something as revolutionary as walking up out of the water and onto the land."

If this book helps you take that next step, writing it will have been more than worthwhile. I invite your comments, stories and experiences online as the journey continues.

Annotated Bibliography
and
Resources for Further Study

Books

Abram, David. *The Spell of the Sensuous*. New York: Vintage Books, 1996. A beautiful exploration into our reciprocal relationship with more-than-human nature.

Barasch, Marc Ian. *Field Notes on the Compassionate Life: A Search for the Soul of Kindness*. Emmaus, PA: Rodale Press, 2005. A touching and compelling book that takes you into the heart and soul of compassion.

Brower, David, Marc Lappe and John Chang McCurdy. *Of All Things Most Yielding*. quoting Tien Tung Hsu. New York: Friends of the Earth/McGraw-Hill,1974.

Chödrön, Pema. *The Places that Scare You: A Guide to Fearlessness in Difficult Times*. Boston: Shambhala, 2002. Thoughtful prose and effective meditative exercises to work with and clear fear receptors.

Fox, Matthew. *Creation Spirituality*. Public lecture at Unity on the Plaza, Kansas City, MO, 1995.

Gilkeson, Jim. *Energy Healing: A Pathway to Inner Growth*. Cambridge, MA: Da Capo Press, 2000.

212

_____ . *A Pilgrim in Your Body: Energy Healing and Spiritual Process*. Bloomington, IN: iUniverse, 2009. Both of these books offer a wealth of exercises to awaken your spiritual qualities. An excellent resource to help you contact, meet and release those receptors that block personal and spiritual development.

Hanh, Thich Nhat. *"Call Me by My True Names."* In Earth Prayers, edited by E. Roberts and E. Amidon. San Francisco: HarperOne, 1991. Beautiful resource for contemplation and prayer.

Heckler, Richard, Ph.D. *Waking up, Alive: The Descent, the Suicide Attempt & The Return to Life.* New York: GP Putnam's Sons, 1994. Sensitive and compassionate exploration of suicide.

Hubbard, Barbara Marx. *One Minute Shift.* Institute of Noetic Sciences, Shift in Action video, 2008. To view video go to www.shiftinaction.com.

Johnson, Steven. *Emergence: The Connected Llives of Ants, Brains, Cities and Software.* New York: Scribner, 2001. Excellent examination of self-organizing systems.

Judith, Anodea. *Waking the Global Heart: Humanity's Rite of Passage from the Love of Power to the Power of Love.* Santa Rosa, CA: Elite Books, 2006. Traces human evolutionary history from the paleolithic to our present global challenge in an artful, clear and engaging way.

Kidd, Sue Monk. *The Secret Life of Bees.* New York: Penguin, 2002. Beautifully written novel that takes you into the subtleties of living with trauma and the power of relationships—with bees and humans—to heal.

Kurtz, Ron. *Body-Centered Psychotherapy: The Hakomi Method.* Mendocino, CA: Life Rhythm, 1990.

_____ and Greg Johanson. *Grace Unfolding: Psychotherapy in the Spirit of the Tao-te-ching.* New York: Bell Tower, 1991. These books offer a wealth of insight, direction and inspiration to help you track and support yourself and your clients through relationship challenges and opportunities.

Levine, Peter A. *Waking the Tiger: Healing Trauma*. Berkeley, CA: North Atlantic Books, 1997. A classic exploration of the nature and neurobiology of trauma which lays the groundwork for the therapeutic practice of Somatic Experiencing.

Lipton, Bruce H. *The Biology of Belief: Unleashing the Power of Consciousness, Matter and Miracles*. Santa Rosa, CA: Love/Elite Books, 2005. More on the wonder of the cell membrane, from the perspective of science and consciousness.

Margulis, Lynn and Dorion Sagan. *What is Sex?* New York: Simon & Schuster, 1997. The biology and history of sex that points us to its evolutionary potential.

McElvaine, Robert S. *Eve's Seed: Biology, the Sexes and the Course of History*. New York: McGraw-Hill, 2001. This book changed the way I look at relationships between men and women. Drawing on many scholarly disciplines, McElvaine creates an exhaustive history of sexual identity and behavior that is insightful and entertaining.

McTaggert, Lynne. *The Intention Experiment*. New York: Free Press, 2007. A compilation of research and guide to the practice and power of intention.

Mitchell, Stephen. *Tao Te Ching: A New English Version*. New York: Harper Perennial Modern Classics, 1991. Classic literature on where the power for change comes from.

Oschman, James. *Energy Medicine: the Scientific Basis*. Edinburgh: Churchill Livingstone, 2000. Scientific description of the cellular matrix and the conductivity of energy between healing partners as well as other scientific foundations of energy medicine.

Penfield, Wilder. *The Mystery of the Mind*. Princeton, NJ: Princeton University Press, 1975. Early scientific exploration on the non-locality of consciousness.

Pert, Candace. *The Molecules of Emotion: The Science Behind Mind-Body Medicine*. New York: Simon & Schuster, 1997. The story of Pert's discovery of neurotransmitter molecules and receptors transmitting emotional messages among cells throughout our body.

Remen, Rachel Naomi. *Kitchen Table Wisdom: Stories that Heal.* New York: Riverhead Books, 1996. Healing wisdom centering on stories shared in interspace.

Sahtouris, Elisabet. *EarthDance; Living Systems in Evolution.* Bloomington, IN: iUniverse, 2000. Evolution beautifully and richly described along with the call to humans to reach our full maturity as a species by awakening to the potential of our global crisis.

Schlitz, Marilyn and Tina Amorok. *Consciousness and Healing: Integral Approaches to Mind-body Medicine.* St. Louis: Churchill Livingstone/Elsevier, 2005. A compilation of the greatest contributors to the articulation, growth and development of an integral vision of healing.

_____ , Cassandra Vieten and Tina Amorak. *Living Deeply: The Art & Science of Transformation in Everyday Life.* Oakland, CA: New Harbinger, 2007. A synthesis of IONS research on transformational practices with wisdom from the world's greatest spiritual traditions. Contains a wealth of exercises to foster your personal healing and transformation.

Shlain, Leonard. *Sex, Time and Power: How Women's Sexuality Shaped Human Evolution.* New York: Viking Penguin, 2003. Another engaging read on our sexual evolution and the opportunity before us.

Taylor, Kylea. *The Ethics of Caring: Honoring the Web of Life in Our Professional Healing Relationships.* Santa Cruz, CA: Hanford Mead, 1995. Taylor takes us through the chakras of our individual and collective bodies to discover the desires, longings and fears that can lead to ethical misconduct. Her approach to working in right relationship to those in non-ordinary states of consciousness is extremely valuable.

Tolle, Eckhart. *A New Earth: Awakening to Your Life's Purpose.*

New York: Penguin/Plume, 2005. Calls humans to awaken to the truth of our own consciousness as the key to personal happiness as well as the ending of conflict and suffering on Earth.

Trager, Milton. As quoted by Deane Juhan in course instruction on New Physiology, Kansas City, MO, 1999.

Twist, Lynne with Teresa Barker. *The Soul of Money: Transforming your Relationship with Money and Life.* New York: W.W. Norton, 2003. See workshops below.

Audio/Video

Goldsworthy, Andy. *Rivers and Tides.* Mediopolis Films, Art and Design; New Video Group, 2004.

Roth, Gabriele and the Mirrors. *Bones.* Raven, 1989. A CD of music to accompany Roth's Five-Waves, rhythms for prayer, transformation and healing through movement and dance.

Available soon on my website

Relationships that Heal slideshow. Color slides of photos and text on DVD which summarize the Cell Membrane Model and Five-step Process for Effective Practice. Good for instructors, especially those looking for a way to present this model to bodywork students.

Ecopsychology of Sexuality. Slideshow exploring the full spectrum of human sexual consciousness with nature as a guide. Helpful tool for workshop leaders and instructors in ecopsychology.

Relationships that Heal Online Course for continuing education in ethics.

Relationships that Heal Blog: A place to bring your challenging practice situations for feedback from the web of professionals who have studied *Relationships that Heal.*

Training Programs/Workshops/Professional Organizations

Relationships That Heal: experiential workshops designed to meet the needs of the various helping professions (social work, psychology, nursing, etc.). Offered regularly as *Trust in Touch* for bodyworkers at the School of Shiatsu and Massage at Harbin Hot Springs, Middletown, CA, and in Italy.

Healing Trauma in Water: an in-depth, experiential training by Diane Tegtmeier and Inika Spence for aquatic bodywork professionals. This course integrates effective trauma healing strategies with the healing potential inherent in aquatic bodywork.

(For other trainings or to schedule a workshop in your area, see my website: http://www.dianetegtmeier.com, or email me at dianetegtmeier@att.net.)

Association for Comprehensive Energy Psychology (ACEP): Provides annual conferences in the US and Canada, support to the field of energy psychology and lists of energy psychology practitioners. Website: www.energypsych.org.

Foundation for Human Enrichment. Education, research and professional training in Somatic Experiencing, a naturalistic approach in healing trauma developed by Dr. Peter Levine, author of *Waking the Tiger* and *Trauma Proofing your Kids.* Boulder, CO. Website: www.traumahealing.com.

Hakomi Institute. Offers training programs in the Hakomi method, body-centered psychotherapy which blends the Eastern traditions of mindfulness and non-violence with Western methodology. Loving presence and the healing relationship are central to Hakomi. Website: www.hakomiinstitute.com.

Institute of Noetic Sciences. International leader in the study of consciousness. Offers workshops, international conferences, *Shift* magazine and the Shift in Action education materials, books, teleconferences and webinars. A great resource for all those interested in actively participating in the evolutionary shift in consciousness and healing. Petaluma, CA. Website: www.noetic.org.

International Community for Ecopsychology (ICE). A public forum for our diverse experiences of the human-nature relationship. Ecopsychology embraces the dissolving boundaries between ecology, psychology and environmental philosophy. ICE offers an e-journal, gatherings, recommended readings, a directory of researchers, practitioners and educators in the field and a blog, called Seeds for Thought, all of which can be accessed from their website: www.ecopsychology.org.

International Society for the Study of Subtle Energy and Energy Medicine (ISSSEEM). A pioneer organization to bridge the boundaries between conventional and energy medicine, science and spirituality. Provides a peer-reviewed journal of research and informational articles, special interest groups and an annual international conference. Arvada, CO. Website: www.issseem.org.

Soul of Money Institute. Offers workshops, keyonote speakers, consulting and coaching for organizations and individuals to create freedom, power and sufficiency in their relationship to money. San Francisco, CA. Website: www.soulofmoney.org.

ACKNOWLEDGMENTS

Like everything in nature, this book grew within a web of relationships. Without the inspiration, support, skill and heart of healing partners, friends, teachers, family and skilled writing professionals, this book would not have found its way into print.

I'm indebted to my teachers in chemistry, physiology and biochemistry: Mr. Rosing, Tommy Dunnagin, and Herb Koepsell who first showed me the wonders of relationships in nature. The writings of early ecologists like Barry Commoner, environmental writers like David Brower and David Abram and spiritual ecologists like Joanna Macy placed those basic science teachings in the context of human relationships with Earth. They all inspired and helped me find spiritual ground. My eco-warrior friends, especially Ron Henricks, Ann Simpson, Wes Jackson, Mari Peterson, and the late Bill Ward, helped me explore what it meant to work with power and love in relationships dedicated to co-creating change.

I'm deeply grateful to the teachers and therapists who have shown me the power of the healing relationship as a container for healing. LeAnn Howard and Bill Carrick modeled an ecological approach to healing relationships that integrated compassion with professional skill. My energy work teacher and healer, Ursula Gilkeson, brought my understanding of healing and the relationships that foster healing into higher dimensions of consciousness and helped me form the spiritual foundation of the work I do today.

Through our struggles with the complexities of a healing partnership, I stretched, grew, ached and learned the power of love in healing.

My greatest teachers, however, have been those who have invited me into their healing processes and became full partners in this mysterious process of healing. They offered me just the right medicine at the right time to awaken me to the power of the cell membrane model to shape my development as a therapist.

Thanks to Andrew Yavelow and Jim Gilkeson, whose honest feedback on early drafts of this book sent me to Hal Zina Bennett, a highly skilled writing mentor. Hal patiently and compassionately showed me how to find my authentic voice with you, the reader in mind. He never gave up—even when I wanted to. Without Hal, this book would have still been a mess of ideas longing to find ground. Deep gratitude also to the group of authors with whom I shared Hal's mentorship. With these 12 women I felt like one lucky cell within a creative body of writers in a very fertile interspace of mutually nurturing ideas. I'm grateful for the feedback they gave me on portions of the book, and a special thanks to Dorothy Von Soest who read the entire manuscript several times and offered invaluable feedback. Finally, it was Dan Barth, my copy editor, who polished the manuscript for publication.

Ruth Richards and I literally watched our ideas mix it up over my kitchen table and find their way through her creative hand into the drawings that distill my words.. I'm so thankful to Ruth for her wisdom, feedback on the manuscript and her ability to express the essence of this book in a single drawing. Thanks to Bob Oertel, my dear son-in-law and professional designer, for his beautiful drawing of the cell, its membrane, and his cover design ideas. Inika Spence added yet another facet to our healing partnership as she collaborated with Ruth, Bob and me to complete the book's interior illustrations. My deep gratitude to this team of artists.

I also want to acknowledge all my friends and colleagues at Harbin Hot Springs, whose love, encouragement and support carried me through this process. Special thanks to Andrew Yavelow, who never failed to ask how my book was doing and then patiently lis-

tened as I told him. Inika supported me as I cried in frustration and despair at ever getting it right. Neil and Madronna understood when I didn't have time to help in the garden, and who put my ideas to work in their relationships with garden helpers. Prem Haskett, Grace Bowman, Will Erme, Eric Richardson and Padma Roy maintained ongoing support and interest in the unfolding of this book. A special thanks, too, for the support and encouragement of the healers I mentor in the Aquatic Energy Healing group.

My daughter Kristen and son Walt listened empathically as I shared my frustrations and expressed relief at the completion of yet another chapter re-write. Beautiful writers themselves, it's been a joy to be supported and cared for by those whose first words and writings brought me such joy. Thanks also to Gary, my beloved friend and former husband, who with Kristen and Walt helped me explore the most challenging and healing relationship of all—the family. I'm also grateful to my children-in-law and love, Stephanie and Bob, for their interest, listening, love and support. My brother Sam's humorous comments and helpful questions lightened the load on the path to publication.

Bella, my first grandchild was born as I began to write this book. Owen, her cousin, was born five months later as I was really getting into the process. Their births, more than anything else, inspired me to continue. It was for them that I was drawn more deeply into the evolutionary potential of the cell membrane model. I could so easily have given up if I didn't feel compelled to do all I could to contribute to a growing consciousness of the sacred interconnected web of life in which these precious beings were now living. By the time Owen's sister Lily was born and Bella's brother Barrett a year later, this book was well on its way. These grandchildren have been my creative spark and my prayer.

My mother's long and difficult dying process accompanied me as I labored to give birth to this book. In her last months and death, I experienced the power of love to heal all wounds, as her body and personality gave way to pure light.

Finally to Jim, my beloved life partner, teacher and best friend, I feel immeasurable gratitude. He suggested I write this book, read the early attempts and risked the perils of honest appraisal. Jim's solid support was unwavering through every emotional explosion when Hal's feedback would arrive in my inbox. When I wanted to give up, Jim listened in a way only another writer and one who loved me could.

Diane Tegtmeier
Middletown, CA
June, 2009